MR. GOODMAN THE PLAYER

Frontispiece to Duffett's *The Empress of Morocco*, 1673; possibly Goodman as "Mariamne a Scinder Wench."
By permission of the Folger Shakespeare Library.

MR. GOODMAN THE PLAYER

John Harold Wilson

University of Pittsburgh Press

Library of Congress Catalog No. 64-16153
Copyright © 1964 by University of Pittsburgh Press

For ROBERT MARK ESTRICH

Preface

In his essay on Sir Walter Scott, Thomas Carlyle wrote: "A Damocles' sword of *Respectability* hangs forever over the poor English Life-Writer (as it does over poor English life in general) and reduces him to the verge of paralysis. Thus it has been said 'there are no English lives worth reading except those of Players, who by the nature of the case have bidden Respectability good-day.'"

Carlyle shared the usual nineteenth-century prejudice against players, not all of whom lacked respectability. He is right, however, in pointing out that the lives of nonrespectable players are interesting. Respectable actors, losing themselves in the characters they create, become as anonymous as musicians in a symphony orchestra. Even if they achieve greatness, their histories are often merely accounts of successive triumphs; their private lives may be completely colorless. Fortunately for the "Life-Writer," many actors bade good day to respectability when they embarked upon the stage, and thereafter they led exciting, unconventional lives.

It is almost impossible to tell the story of a reputable Restoration player unless, like R. W. Lowe in his famous *Thomas Betterton*, one uses his subject as a peg on which to hang a history of the stage. Even for the choice and master spirits of the age, the normal sources of dramatic biography—records, memoirs, letters, diaries, dramatic reviews, and anecdotes—are lacking or in very short supply. But the disreputable player, who may have left no sublime footprints on the sands of time, at least smudged them in his progress. One can trace his trail.

In the following pages Cardell Goodman serves a double function. As a member of the King's Company of Comedians from 1673 to its death in 1682 he is a useful peg on which to hang an account of the decline and fall of a famous repertory company. He was also the antithesis of respectability, an attractive rogue whose escapades would furnish material for a picaresque romance. I will not apologize for him. He was what he was.

For assistance in gathering material for this study I am indebted to Dr. Louis B. Wright and the trustees of the Folger Shakespeare Library; to Professor Robert M. Estrich and the officers of the Ohio State University; to Mr. F. P. White, Keeper of the Records of St. John's College, Cambridge; to Mr. Arthur G. Hudd of the British Museum; and to the staffs of the Folger Library, the British Museum, and the Public Record Office. For suggestions, criticisms, and corrections I am deeply grateful to Professor Richard D. Altick and Louise Walker Wilson.

J. H. W.

Contents

I	Study to Stage	1
II	The King's Company	13
III	The War of the Theatres	33
IV	The Lean Years	49
V	Decline and Fall	65
VI	Barbara	82
VII	Libels and Lampoons	97
VIII	To Kill a King	111
IX	The Epilogue	128
	Notes	136
	Index	147

Illustrations

Frontispiece—"Mariamne a Scinder Wench"	Facing	iii
Barbara, Duchess of Cleveland	Facing	87
Stenographical Map of the Second Theatre Royal & Vicinity	Facing	118

I

Study to Stage

Forgetful of gray March skies and London's smoke and fog, the audience in the Theatre Royal waited eagerly for the play to begin. Drawn by reports that the famous actor Cardell Goodman had agreed to perform gratis for the benefit of the "young" players (the hirelings of the United Company), the ladies and gentlemen of Court and Town had braved the raw cold of a spring afternoon to pack the theatre. Goodman had retired from the stage, but he was still young, handsome enough to be called a "modern Adonis," and a notable performer in heroic roles.

The golden light of the wax candles in chandeliers over the stage picked out a patchwork of green and crimson, silver and blue—the gowns of the ladies and the gold-laced coats of the gentlemen. The beaux in their great blonde periwigs jiggled on the backless benches of the pit, bantered with the orange-girls, made assignations with doxies in vizard masks, and ogled the bare-bosomed beauties in the boxes. In the King's box sat Dowager Queen Catherine (widow of King Charles the Second) with her ladies in waiting. Backstage in the tiring room, John Downes, the prompter, was rapidly losing his mind. It was past time for the play to begin, and Goodman refused to let the curtains be drawn until his mistress, Barbara Palmer, Duchess of Cleveland, arrived. The actresses in their copper-lace finery shivered and tittered; the actors swore steadily.

Time passed while the audience wondered, stamped, and called for action. Queen Catherine sent a messenger backstage with a peremptory order for the play to begin at once. "Damme," said

Goodman, "I care not if the playhouse be filled with queens from top to bottom. I will not tread the stage until my duchess comes." Just then a breathless doorkeeper rushed in, crying that the Duchess of Cleveland had arrived at last. The curtains rose, the Prologue stepped out to a blare of trumpets, the play began, and Cardell Goodman gave his usual magnificent performance. Or so the story goes.[1]

That day Goodman acted Alexander in a revival of Nathaniel Lee's *The Rival Queens*, a part he had played with such success in the years before he left the stage as to earn for him the affectionate title "Alexander the Great." Other actors were successful in the role, notably Charles Hart, Will Mountfort, Jack Verbruggen, and the great Thomas Betterton himself, but none ever played it with Goodman's grace and harmony, and only he became so completely identified with it that to name the character was to recall the actor. Betterton, in his old age, testified to Goodman's skill. Discussing the importance of smoothness in acting, he said, "I remember, among many, an Instance in the Madness of Alexander the Great, in Lee's Play. Mr. Goodman always went through it with all the Force the Part requir'd, and yet made not half the Noise as some who succeeded him; who were sure to bellow it out in such a manner that their Voice would fail them before the End, and lead them to such a languid and ennervate Hoarseness, as entirely wanted that agreeable Smoothness . . . which is the perfection of beautiful Speaking."[2]

Cardell Goodman, tall, handsome, debonaire, and fond of elegant dress, was a master of "agreeable Smoothness." Regrettably, he was also notable as a spendthrift, a gambler, a wencher, a highwayman, an associate of clippers and coiners, an alleged poisoner, a duchess's paramour, a conspirator, an evidence, and a fugitive. He lived a busy life.

Although he left the stage in 1684, when he was barely thirty-one years old, and performed only occasionally for a few years after that date, Cardell was popularly known for the rest of his life as either "Alexander the Great" or "Mr. Goodman, the player." In 1707, ten years after Cardell had fled to France, a scurrilous poet in *The Dutchess of C[leveland]'s Memorial* represented the Duchess as saying,

> Poor Rowley being dead and gone
> I howl'd and had Remorse Sir,
> To comfort me scum Goodman came
> Whom I made Master Horser.

From this single instance, Thomas Macaulay leaped to the conclusion that Cardell was "popularly called 'Scum Goodman,' " and by that epithet he has been forever damned. Of course Macaulay was a nineteenth century Whig, and Goodman a seventeenth century Jacobite—a Tory supporter of the Stuart cause after the Revolution of 1689. Anyone who opposed Macaulay's hero, King William the Third, was obviously a scoundrel to be vilified.[3]

Whatever else Goodman may have been, he was at least a gentleman, if not to the manner born. In 1714 his first biographer, Theophilus Lucas, described him as a "memorable Esquire . . . the son of a parson of Shaftesbury in Dorsetshire, where he received his Birth." Lucas was right in one respect: Cardell's father was a parson.

One of Cardell's great-grandfathers, John Goodman of Cumberlow Green, and one of his grandfathers, John Goodman of Ware, were substantial country gentlemen who had held at one time or another the manors of Blakesware, Cumberlow Green, and Rushden in the north of Hertfordshire. Another great-grandfather, Thomas Cardell, had been a Gentleman of the Privy Chamber to both Queen Elizabeth and Queen Anne, consort of King James the First. One of Thomas Cardell's daughters, Grace, had married John Goodman of Ware; another, Anne, had married John Toppe, a gentleman of Wiltshire.

Cardell's father, Cardell Goodman, senior, as the second son of John of Ware and therefore obliged to make his own way in the world, chose the path of learning and religion. Matriculating first at Oxford—where he signed himself "armiger" (i.e., esquire)—he quickly migrated to Cambridge, graduated from Emmanuel College, became a fellow of St. John's College, took an M.A. in 1629, a B.D. in 1636, and was duly ordained.

According to the pleasant custom of those days, a young clergyman could remain a tutor and fellow indefinitely while waiting his turn for appointment to a good living, so long as he avoided the mousetrap of matrimony. In 1641, when Mr. Goodman was appointed rector of Freshwater and Brook in the Isle of Wight, he was thirty-three years old, a studious man, blindly loyal to Church and King and, as the result of an artistic streak in his cosmos, given to writing "Sacred meditations and private ejaculations digested into verse"—limping imitations of the great George Herbert.

All Saints, Freshwater, was, and is, a fine old thirteenth century church, overlooking the main road leading to the village. The living (in the gift of the Master, Fellows, and Scholars of St. John's College) was one of the richest in the island, capable of supporting both a rector and a curate. When Mr. Goodman arrived, the incumbent curate was John Hooke, father of three children, the youngest of whom, six-year-old Robert, was to become a famous virtuoso and Curator of the Royal Society. The friendship established in these early years between the Hooke and Goodman families was to be important in shaping the career of Cardell, junior.

Although Mr. Goodman, senior, was now free to marry, there is no reason to believe that he did so at once. Instead he seems to have taken under his roof his widowed aunt, Mrs. Anne Toppe, to whom he dedicated his unpublished "Sacred Meditations." When she died in 1648 he celebrated her departure by putting up in his church a plaque with an epitaph of his own composition pointing out that Mrs. Toppe "In Flames of Zeale did upwards rowle." After he recovered from this fine frenzy he married. All we know about his wife is that her name was Katherine.[4]

During the troubled years of the Civil War, while Cavalier and Roundhead burned and pillaged impartially until the Roundheads won and sent King Charles the First to the block, Mr. Goodman was safe enough in his remote little village under the sweep of the great downs. But after Cromwell set up his protectorate the stubborn clergyman refused to sign the Covenant and to take the oaths of allegiance to the new government. The result was that in March, 1651, the Council of State ejected him from his living as "dangerous to the Commonwealth." Mr. Goodman took his wife and his household goods across the Solent to Southampton. There, in October or November, 1653, his only son was born, and there, in March, 1654, Cardell Goodman, senior, died.[5]

Some time after that event, Katherine Goodman took her son to Cambridge, thirty miles from her husband's family home at Ware, Hertfordshire. As soon as Cardell, junior, was old enough, she sent him to Mr. Thomas Wyborrow's school in Cambridge, where he learned his letters, his catechism, and the fundamentals of Latin grammar. He was six years old in May, 1660, when the Mayor of Cambridge proclaimed King Charles the Second in the Market Square, and a squad of soldiers on the roof of King's College chapel "gave a volley of shott." There were "great expressions and acclamations of Joy from all sorts." Cardell was eleven in April, 1665, when a press gang came to the little town on the edge of the watery fens and took "out of Cambr betweene 3 and 4 score" men for "His Maties service against the Dutch." Two months later, when the Dutch and English fleets came to death grips in the Channel, he could hear all day long "the noyse of gunns in the Ayre."

That summer the Great Plague came to London. On September 1, so that Londoners would not carry the plague to Cambridge, King Charles forbade the holding of Stourbridge Fair. The dread pestilence arrived nonetheless. The university closed down until the following spring, and Isaac Newton, a fellow of Trinity College, retired to the country, watched the fall of an apple, and opened a new door to the marble halls of science.[6]

Young Cardell was either precocious or remarkably industrious. Although the usual age for matriculation at one of the universities was sixteen to eighteen, he was just "past thirteen" when, on November 30, 1666, he passed an examination in Latin grammar and won admission to his father's college, St. John's, Cambridge. The fact that he was listed on the college books as a "pensioner"—one who paid his own expenses—suggests that his family still had some means. He was assigned to a tutor, "Dominus" John Saywell, who, like Peter Gunning, then Master of the college, was a strong loyalist. Some part, at least, of Cardell's later Jacobitism may be traced to his impressionable youth at college.

Presumably Cardell's life behind the mellow brick walls of St.

John's was much like that of any seventeenth-century student. He must have made friends, but few of his companions are remembered by posterity. Lewis Maidwell, who took an M.A. at St. John's in 1671, eventually became well known as the master of a private school in London, and even wrote a successful play, *The Loving Enemies* (1680). Infamous Titus Oates was first admitted to Caius College as a sizar (a servitor or attendant) on June 29, 1667. "The plague and he," said a fellow student with a jaundiced but faulty memory, "visited the university in the same year." On February 2, 1669, Titus transferred to St. John's. Fortunately he was quickly "sent down" (dismissed) for cheating a tailor, and Cambridge was spared granting a degree to one of the greatest liars in all history.[7]

From the *Memoirs* of Robert Bruce, Earl of Ailesbury (written 1728–32), we learn that Cardell "began to study well," an assertion which is supported by the fact that on November 4, 1667, he was admitted to a scholarship. His education, of course, was expected to lead him in his father's footsteps. To a young gentleman with neither money nor patrons the Church offered an assured career, and Cambridge, like Oxford, prided itself upon its production of priests. Although the old scholasticism was rapidly breaking down, its forms were still observed at the universities, in spite of the new science and the corrosive materialism of Thomas Hobbes. Scholarship and godliness walked hand in hand, and the budding clergyman had his faith fortified by logic and rhetoric.[8]

Admittedly, it is hard to picture Cardell Goodman creeping with a shining morning face to prayers, sermons, lectures, and disputations, and late at night reading theology by the light of a tallow dip. We may be sure that, like most of his fellows, he spent a deal of time roaming the fens, hunting and fishing, and, when the weather served, playing games or swimming in the Cam. Of course there were holidays during the terms, especially when distinguished visitors came, and town and gown turned out to welcome them, the dons in their scarlet robes and flat caps, the scholars in the colors of their colleges.

In May, 1669, for instance, Cosmo de' Medici, Prince of Tuscany ("a proper man, very thick in person & very swarthy in his favour"), came for a short visit and was entertained with Latin addresses, a dinner, and a Latin play in "ye Comedy house" at Trinity College. In October, 1670, the Duke of York and his lovely duchess, Maria D'Estes, stopped overnight at the New England Inn on their way to Newmarket. With them in their coach was Barbara Palmer, recently created Duchess of Cleveland, but better known by her earlier title, Lady Castlemaine. Barbara was still the King's mistress *en titre* and famous as the most beautiful woman in all England. It is unlikely that young Cardell, lost in a crowd of gawking undergraduates, even dreamed of some day meeting the regal, blue-eyed, bronze-haired courtesan on equal terms, much less of sleeping with her. Next day beauty departed in a cloud of dust and liveried horsemen. A month later came William, Prince of Orange ("a well-countenanced man a smooth and smeeger face and a handsome head of hayre of his owne"), whose life was to impinge on Cardell's with tragic force. Finally, on October 4, 1671, dark, saturnine King Charles himself came over from Newmarket for the day. The town gave him "100 twenty shilling peeces of broad gold in a crimson coullered velvet or good plush purse with gold fringe and gold strings." The university entertained him with speeches, a dinner, and "a comedy called 'All is Mistaken,' with dancing and singing performed with great applause." Since the comedy was "Acted by the Schollers," it is tempting to suggest that Cardell Goodman carried a role, but the names of the players are forever lost.[9]

Cambridge had other pleasant distractions. There was Stourbridge Fair, for example, where in August and September the scholars could see plays produced by a company of strolling actors. There was Kirk's coffee house in Market Street, where the indolent repaired after breakfast to talk, smoke, and read Muddiman's latest newsletter. There were taverns such as the Three Tuns at the corner of St. Edward's Passage, and the Rose near Trinity Street, where the scholars could get their fill of cakes and ale. Then there were bawdy-houses. For many young collegians it was an easy step from adolescence to adultery. Cambridge was much like Oxford, where at this time there were "Baudy houses and light huswifes giving divers young men the pox soe that that disease is very common among them and some obscure pocky doctors obtaine a living by it, and whereas it was notorious formerly to those that had it, it is now soe common . . . that they glory of it."[10]

There is no reason to believe that Cardell ever held virtue dear. Years later Tom D'Urfey created for him the dramatic character of Townly, "a Modish inconstant young fellow, in Love with, and beloved by all Women," in a comedy, *Sir Barnaby Whigg*. In the course of the play, Wilding, another young rake, asks, "Is Townly a modest fellow . . . ?" "Modest!" replies Townly's friend Benedict, "Pox on him. I knew a surgeon that cur'd him of two Claps when he was at Cambridge." This is hardly material for biography, but to an audience which knew Goodman well and knew that he was the only Cantabrigian in the company, the jest must have had point.

Whatever his extra-curricular amusements, in four years Cardell managed to load up enough learned lumber to pass the required examinations in Grammar, Rhetoric, Logic, Ethics, Metaphysics, Natural Philosophy, and Geometry, and to take a degree early in 1671, at the age of seventeen. Now he had to decide on a career. Prudence (and his father's family) would recommend further residence at the university, a master's degree, and a life of celibate pedagogy or wedded priesthood. Instead, some time in the months following his degree, while he lingered on at Cambridge, Cardell discovered (says Ailesbury) that "he preferred a stage life."

His reasons for the choice are obscure, but it seems likely that to a youth of adventurous spirit, a lover of gaiety and finery, the drabness of the life of learning had no appeal. Moreover, many a young collegian, after reading Hobbes' *Leviathan*, lost his faith in the power of the spirit and came to agree with the Hobbist poet, Lord Rochester, that the universities, devoted to metaphysics, "an Ignis fatuus of the Mind," were no more than "Reverend Bedlams" filled with "frantic Crouds of thinking Fools." Accepting materialism, they came to agree too that

> *Thoughts were giv'n for Actions Government;*
> *Where Action ceases, Thought's impertinent.*
> *Our Sphere of Action is Life's happiness,*
> *And he that thinks beyond, thinks like an Ass.*

From this it was an easy step to the conclusion that the sole end of life was pleasure: women, wit, and song. The wine was taken for granted.

In addition, the air of Restoration England was full of change and ferment. Young men of gentle birth and good education were having spectacular careers as diplomats on the continent; as commanders of frigates guarding convoys against the Algerine pirates; as factors in the Levant; as merchants in Lombard Street; as soldiers, courtiers, and lawyers. Why not as an actor? The strolling players who regularly visited Cambridge could paint for Cardell a highly colored picture of the glamor and rewards of the stage. They could point to the wealth and fame of the great actor Charles Hart, leading man of the King's Company, who had been the first lover of little Nell Gwyn, now one of the King's mistresses, and who had recently shared with his Majesty the boudoir favors of Lady Castlemaine. They could point to handsome William Smith of the Duke's House, whose possible punishment was much bemoaned by the Court ladies when he killed his man in a duel. (He escaped scot-free.) Then there was Henry Harris, also of the Duke's House, Yeoman of the Revels, very acceptable at Court, and a boon companion of The Wits, the titled elegants who had set themselves up as the arbiters of wit and drama. Only recently Jo Haynes (an ex-Oxonian), a comedian at the King's House, had gone to France in the train of the Duke of Buckingham, and by his mimicry and dancing had won the applause and gifts of the French court. Cardell was talented, young, and handsome, with "a brown or Nutmeg-Complexion." Why should he not try the stage?[11]

If his reasons for giving up learning are obscure, the immediate occasion for his leaving Cambridge is even more so. Colley Cibber, Goodman's great admirer, tells us that one day in 1696 he met the famous actor at dinner. After dinner, "Goodman, without Disguise or sparing himself, fell into a laughing account of several loose Passages of his younger Life; as his being expelled the University of Cambridge for being one of the hot-headed sparks who were accused in the cutting and defacing of the Duke of Monmouth's Picture, then Chancellor of that place." Either Cibber's memory betrayed him (he was writing some forty years after the event), and Goodman described some unrecorded episode during the chancellorship of Edward Montague, Earl of Manchester (1660–1671), or Goodman was spinning a fine yarn. Actors love to dramatize their lives. The fact is that Monmouth did not become chancellor of Cambridge until July 15, 1674, nearly two years after Goodman had left the university.[12]

Theophilus Lucas is even more confused. Lacking facts, he filled the gap between Cardell's graduation and his first appearance on the stage with fantasy and fable. Goodman, said Lucas, "having [a] good education bestow'd upon him, came up to London when he was about 20 years of age, where he was made one of the Pages of the Backstairs to King Charles II." Regrettably, although the last statement is slavishly repeated by all subsequent writers, there is no record of such an unlikely appointment in the annals of the Court. But it may be worth noting that a certain Lowde Cordell was sworn in as a page in ordinary on November 29, 1672. The similarity of names may have misled Mr. Lucas.[13]

We may take his further account of Goodman's younger days as the usual fiction invented by hack biographers to pad out their lives of the famous and infamous. Goodman (said Lucas) was a page for about three years; then his father died, leaving him "2,000 Pounds in Money but no real Estate." (How a parson acquired such wealth, Lucas does not say.) Cardell, with the modern equivalent of $40,000 in his pockets, became acquainted "with the greatest Rakes in Town, and being very extravagant, as well as neglectful of his Business, he lost his Place, and in less than 2 years was as poor as Job."

However (Lucas continued), the handsome young prodigal, who was still dressed in the height of fashion, was very attractive to feminine eyes. One day in the Strand he met "a very fine Woman," who, "with an Amorous Leer," invited him into a tavern, took him to an upstairs room, plied him with food and drink, and sang him to sleep. When he awoke an hour or two later, he found a bed in the room, "let through a Trap-door in the Ceiling, by Cords and Pulleys, for this it seems was the private Nursery Chamber of Venus. By this, Goodman was farther confirm'd in what she aim'd at, and could not be so uncivil as not to gratifie her Desires in so pleasing a way; insomuch that she prevail'd with him to sleep in her Arms for that Night." When he awoke the next morning, the gentlewoman—possibly a young wife who, because her husband was old and impotent, "wanted an Heir to an Estate"—had departed, leaving behind as a token of her gratitude a silver-wire purse containing a hundred guineas!

For some weeks thereafter Cardell "lived as merry as a Fox, that had stored his Hole with the Spoils of a Henroost." At last came the day when his stud-fee was spent, wasted away "like Butter stoping the Crannies of a hot Oven." Without a farthing in his pockets, our hero marched into a cook's shop and "filled his Belly to the Tune of about Twenty or Two and Twenty Pence for Meat, Bread, and Drink."

When it came time to pay the reckoning, Goodman called the cook aside and said, "Landlord, I have a great Secret to deliver to you, which I would not have you to divulge for the World." When the cook had vowed secrecy, Goodman explained, "Why, truly, Landlord, I am a Gentleman's Son, come of a very good Family, but through Misfortunes I am at present reduced to a very mean State; and have not any Money to pay for what I have called [for]; but, as you said you would keep my Secret, I hope you will be as good as your Word, in saying nothing of it to any Person."

Because his vow kept the cook from calling the watch, he had to accept his loss with what grace he could muster. But as Goodman was strolling toward the door, the cook pulled up his apron and gave the gentleman "a good kick o' the Breech." "You may go about your Business now," said the cook, "but for the future, Sir, I would desire the favor of you never to declare any more of your Secrets to me, for if you do, upon my word, Sir, I shall never keep them."[14]

Of course such anecdotes as these are useless for biography, but at least they testify to Goodman's reputation as wencher, spendthrift, and adventurer; they could be based on actual events, colored and enlarged in the retelling. Nature intended Cardell to play a picaresque role, with fame outrunning performance. His reputation (if not the anecdotes) is confirmed by Cibber, who listened happily to Goodman's lurid reminiscences and concluded that his adventures "had not disqualified him for the Stage, which, like the Sea Service, refuses no Man for his Morals that is able-bodied." Goodman was not only able-bodied; he was a gentleman by birth and a university graduate—a note above the common cry of players.

Although we do not know the details about Cardell's traverse from the study to the stage we can be reasonably sure that he came to London late in November, 1672. It was a bad time in which to leave the safety of Cambridge for the perils of the city. The roads were infested with highwaymen. England was in the midst of its third war of the century with Holland. The Fleet had been laid up for the winter, but, as usual, the unpaid sailors were starving, and roaming the streets in bands. Trade was at a standstill, prices were rising, and London was in a bad humor, aggravated by a cold, wet, sickly autumn. The narrow, twisting streets were slick and black with rain. The shop signs creaked in a bitter northwest wind.

At Gresham College in Bishopgate Street, where the Royal Society met and its curator had his lodgings, Robert Hooke, a crooked little bachelor with a pale face and popping gray eyes, went about his affairs, preparing experiments for the Society, and, in his other capacity as Surveyor of London, "viewing" sites for new construction. On the evening of November 29, with an eye toward lechery, he had supper early, stoked up his fireplaces, and afterward went to bed with his maidservant, Nell Young. (In his *Diary* Hooke marked such episodes with the sign of Pisces, thus: "Nell ♓.") Later that night he was disturbed by a knocking at his front door. The next day he noted in his *Diary*, "Goodman here from Cambridge, not let in." No wonder.

To judge from the later appearance of Goodman's name in Hooke's laconic *Diary*—a collection of memoranda rather than a narrative—a day or so afterward the young man was "let in" and befriended for his father's sake. Hooke knew many people who could be useful to an aspirant for the stage, among them Sir Christopher Wren the architect; Robert Streeter, famous as a painter of stage scenery; Thomas Betterton the actor; and Charles Killigrew son of Thomas Killigrew, Master of the King's Company. Some time in the spring of 1673 Cardell was admitted into the ranks of the King's Company.[15]

II

The King's Company

In 1672 the fortunes of the King's Company of Comedians were at low tide. Once a band of distinguished players, so proud and rich as to arouse the envy of the King's courtiers, it had lost much of its strength by death and retirement. Most of the men who had started out so gallantly in 1660 under the mastership of Thomas Killigrew were experienced actors who had performed at the Blackfriars, the Cockpit, or the Red Bull before the closing of the theatres in 1642.

Shortly after the Restoration of King Charles the Second they adapted for theatrical use Gibbon's enclosed tennis court in Lincoln's Inn Fields, where with new scenes and pretty actresses they caught the fancy of the Town. In 1663 they built the splendid Theatre Royal between Bridges Street and Drury Lane in Covent Garden. There for nine years the wits and beaux of the Town, the virgins, viragoes, and vizard-masks resorted every afternoon (except Sunday) to applaud the heroics of handsome Charles Hart, the tender love-making of Edward Kynaston, the character-acting of Michael Mohun and William Cartwright, the villainy of Nicholas Burt, the follies of Robert Shatterall and William Wintershall, and the excellent dancing of that consummate artist and comedian John Lacy.

Now (with the exception of Kynaston, who was barely thirty) the master players, shareholders in both theatre building and company, were all in their fifties and sixties—old men for the seventeenth century, subject to aches, catarrhs, gouts, and rheums. But in spite of their ailments, the master players clung grimly to their posts, quarreled regularly with Thomas Killigrew, grudged hiring new actors and actresses, hoarded their shillings, and kept all the best parts for themselves. The younger players of the only other "patent" company in London, the Duke of York's Comedians at Lisle's tennis court in Lincoln's Inn Fields, at first overshadowed by the King's Company, had now reached maturity, and had recently built an even more magnificent theatre (at the cost of £9,000) in Dorset Garden on the riverbank east of the Temple. It was reported that King Charles liked the new playhouse so much that "he hath given the players £1,000 towards the building of it." Now, under the authority of Lady Davenant (vice Sir William, who had died in 1668) and the able leadership of young Thomas Betterton and Henry Harris, the Duke's Company was getting the pick of the new plays, the applause of Court and Town, and most of the profits.[1]

To make matters much worse for the King's Company, about eight o'clock on the night of January 25, 1672, a fire started in the Theatre Royal under the stairs, where Mrs. Mary Meggs ("Orange Moll") the fruit-seller kept her wares. Undetected, it burned through to the scene room, and then, fed by "the Scenes, compos'd of oyl and porous Firr," it spread so rapidly that within minutes it raged out of control, devouring most of the theatre, all the scenes, properties, books, and costumes, and spreading to adjoining houses in Russell Street, Vinegar Yard, and Drury Lane. Experienced fire-fighters stopped its progress by blowing up houses with gunpowder, and in one such explosion succeeded in blowing up also a promising young actor, Mr. Richard Bell. By midnight the Theatre Royal was in ruins. The stricken company lost a building which had cost at least £2,400, plus one expendable actor, and scenes, properties, and costumes acquired at great cost over the past twelve years. The theatre's neighbors lost also: some fifty or sixty shops and houses were burned or blown up. Even literature suffered when an unknown poetaster bemoaned "The Unhappy Conflagration of the Theatre Royal," calling to his fellow poets,

> *Ungrateful Rhymers! can you silent see*
> *The Royal Stage sink in this Tragedy,*
> *And not Condole its Fate in some sweet strain,*
> *Amphion-like, may Build it up again?*

> *Have you forgot the Third-dayes Profit clear,*
> *Which for a new-vampt Play kept you a Year!*
> *You brisk Town-Gallants, whom Common Esteem*
> *Hath voted Wits, or at least such would seem,*
> *Can you behold the Belov'd Fabrick burn,*
> *And not bestow an Epitaph on'ts Urne?*[2]

Before the ashes were cold, the King's Players, with no time for epitaphs or urns, were hard at work. Lisle's tennis court, vacant since the Duke's Company had deserted it, was available—a grim, barnlike structure with a primitive stage, but at least a shelter until a new theatre could be built. The desperate King's Players scraped together their available cash, refurbished the musty old tennis court, and opened it on February 26 with a revival of Beaumont and Fletcher's *Wit without Money*, a timely selection. When the proscenium curtains went up, the audience saw all the actors on the stage "in Melancholick postures." Then sturdy Michael Mohun stepped out and delivered a prologue written especially for the occasion by John Dryden. Comparing the actors to shipwrecked travelers surviving on a barren shore, Mohun thanked the spectators for their noble charity in coming, protested against the fanatic notion that the fire was "a Judgment on the Stage," and promised that as London had risen more splendid from the Great Fire of 1666, so a new and perhaps even more magnificent theatre would arise from the ashes of the Theatre Royal.[3]

Vain prophecy! Because the King, deeply in debt, had stopped payments from the Exchequer on January 2, the goldsmiths were unwilling to lend money for a new building. The King's Company could barely scrape along in the old Lincoln's Inn theatre and could put aside nothing for a new theatre. Lack of scenes, machines, and costumes made it impossible to mount the spectacular shows demanded by the many-headed monster of the pit. The true wits—intellectuals who loved dramatic artistry for its own sake—came when they could, but many were drawn away by preparations for a new war with Holland. Fashionable playgoers preferred the magnificence of the new Duke's Theatre, and the playwrights who were not under contract to the King's Company chose to offer their best plays to the opposition.

Easter and Trinity terms (April 24 to June 26 in 1672) went

by with only one poor new play, Shipman's *Henry the Third of France*, at the temporary Theatre Royal. Ordinarily these two terms "were times for great resort of Gentry & psons of quality" to the theatres. The law courts in Westminster Hall were going full blast; usually Parliament was in its spring session; and country gentlemen brought their families to town to buy clothes, goggle at the king while he ate his dinner in the Banqueting Hall, and laugh or weep at the newest plays. This year the prosperous Duke's Company drew the crowds with two new comedies and a new spectacle-melodrama, Crowne's *The History of Charles the Eighth*. In May the King's Company scored in its turn with Dryden's best comedy, *Marriage à la Mode*, but its run was topped in June by the great success of Ravenscroft's *The Citizen Turn'd Gentleman* ("Mamamouchi") at the Duke's House. This wild, ridiculous farce ran nine days consecutively and was revived again and again in succeeding months. The country bumpkins and the empty-headed fops in the pit loved it, and loved to quote its nonsense phrases, "Hullibabilah da," "Marabarah sahem," and "Chu, chu, chu."[4]

In 1672 the "Long Vacation" of the law courts ran from June 27 to October 23. Ordinarily in the Vacation the King took his family and Court to Hampton Court or Windsor Castle. With Parliament adjourned, the gentry took their families to their country houses; the rural squires fled to their dairies and haymows; and Londoners, eager for sunshine and air, preferred the walks of St. James's Park, the arbors of the Mulberry Garden, or the green glades of Vauxhall to the hot, close theatres.

Usually in the Long Vacation the managers of both patent companies closed down their theatres for weeks at a time. Sometimes they tried out new plays which could be cheaply mounted, or gave their "hirelings"—all the women and those lesser players who, like the women, were paid weekly salaries—chances to play leading roles in revivals while the sharing actors were off on holiday. This summer, with England and Holland at war and the Fleet at sea again after the great Battle of Solebay (May 28), London was emptier than usual. The master players of the King's Company, busy with their building affairs, gave leave to the hireling actresses to play for their own profit, to present a series of stock plays "acted all by women." In rapid succession the women put on Dryden's *Secret Love*, Killigrew's *The Parson's Wedding*, Beaumont and Fletcher's *Philaster*, and at least one other risqué drama. The performances were made doubly piquant by the fact that dark, handsome Rebecca Marshall, blonde little Betty Boutell, and pretty Anne Reeve (said to be John Dryden's mistress) played in breeches and spoke immodest prologues and epilogues. In tripping couplets they sneered at the absent master players as old and impotent, boasted that their own legs were "no ill sight," and hinted at their carnal availability by protesting that they were not at all like the female impersonators of an earlier age:

> *They went but Females to the Tyring-room,*
> *While we, in kindness to our selves and you,*
> *Can hold out Women to our Lodgings too.*

From one epilogue we learn that there was talk of joining the two companies into one—ten years before the event.[5]

While the women were shaking their legs in Lisle's tennis court, preparations for rebuilding the Theatre Royal went on. The master players, seeking anxiously for cash, petitioned the King "for payment of the arrears due them" at the rates of £10 for each of his Majesty's visits to the theatre, £20 when he brought the Queen and her maids, and £20 for each command performance at Whitehall. They begged also "for assistance in rebuilding their theatre, which will cost £2,000 more than the old one." They insisted that without help they could not go on with the new building and at the same time "pay for clothes, scenes, &c, for their now acting at Lincolns Inn Fields." There is no record of royal largess. Instead, his Majesty, in serious straits himself with an expensive war on his hands, told the players to trim down their estimate and figure on "a Plain Built House." On April 30, 1674 (after the war had ended) the King authorized payment of the arrears due the players from April 15, 1667, to June, 1673. The various warrants for payment totalled £1,930, but in Restoration England it was usually a far cry from the King's warrant to the Treasurer's cash.[6]

Some historians assert that in lieu of an outright gift King Charles ordered a "church brief"—a letter authorizing collections in parish churches—for the relief of the King's Company. He ordered such a brief indeed, but in the form usual after all public calamities—fires, floods, and epidemics—and the money to be collected was designed to aid ALL the victims of the Theatre Royal fire, not merely the players. Collections began in the summer of 1672 and were still being taken up as late as March, 1674. Probably the sum amassed was not large. Most country churches gave only a few shillings apiece, and only the wealthy London churches gave substantial amounts. Whatever share may have come at last to the players, it was less than a farthing to the pound of their needs.

Eventually the players were forced to mortgage the ground on which the old Theatre Royal had stood. Various private investors were found, who agreed to put up most of the money for a new playhouse, the actors to supply a part. An architect was chosen, the foundation stone was laid, and the slow process of rebuilding was under way.[7]

In October, 1672, the court came back to London from Newmarket, where the sports-loving King spent part of every spring and fall at the races. Gentlemen brought their families back to town; health-seekers returned from Bath and Epsom Wells; Members of Parliament came from all parts of the kingdom; sailors returned from sea duty, and soldiers from the endless wars in Flanders. By Michaelmas Term (October 23) the Town was full and the theatres were "up" again.

Usually, at the beginning of a winter season, the theatres tried to catch the favor of the Town with a new play or the revival of a recent hit. In 1672 the Duke's Company had both: Henry Neville Payne's lively new comedy, *The Morning Ramble,* and Ravenscroft's durable *Citizen Turn'd Gentleman.* The King's Comedians had to be content to warm up stale fare. However, John Dryden, bound by contract to the King's Company, finished his new comedy, *The Assignation,* in time for a November production. Unfortunately "it succeeded ill in the representation" in spite of a clever prologue delivered by Jo Haynes, a comedian with the face of a gargoyle, scoring the opposition company's still popular "Mamamouchi." Almost on the heels of Dryden's failure, Thomas Shadwell heaped the steaming ordure of the

Duke's Company stage with his bawdy comedy, *Epsom Wells*, a play which King Charles saw at the playhouse on December 2 and 4 and commanded for a Whitehall performance on December 27. Possibly it was the first play seen by Cardell Goodman after his arrival in London.[8]

Suffering in pride and pocket, the King's Comedians struggled on through the winter of 1672-73, almost succumbing to a low blow in January, when a French troupe arrived in London and set up their stage in a private theatre at York House in the Strand, an ancient palace rented by the French Ambassador. Although the Frenchmen charged standard admission prices and had only a primitive stage and sketchy scenes, they had the merit of novelty, and everyone attracted by their big red "bills" posted about town had to see them at least once. For a while their competition hurt both the patent companies, but in February the Duke's House produced an operatic version of *Macbeth*, with songs, spectacular scenes, and new machines. This, followed by two successful comedies, drew the crowds in spite of the foreign competition at York House. The Theatre Royal, strained to its limits, could manage only a weak new comedy, Thomas Duffett's *The Spanish Rogue*, and a revival of an old play, Carlell's *Arviragus and Philicia*. In his prologue to the latter, Dryden complained that

> *With sickly Actors and an old House too,*
> *We're match'd with Glorious Theatres and New,*
> *And with our Alehouse Scenes, and Cloaths bare worn,*
> *Can neither raise Old Plays, nor New adorn.*
> *If all these ills could not undo us quite,*
> *A Brisk French Troop is grown your dear delight,*
> *Who with broad bloody Bills call you each day,*
> *To laugh, and break your Buttons at their Play.*
> *Or see some serious Piece, which we presume*
> *Is fal'n from some incomparable Plume;*
> *And therefore, Messieurs, if you'l do us grace,*
> *Send Lacquies early to preserve your Place . . .*
> *Mean time we Languish, and neglected lye,*
> *Like Wives, while You keep better Company;*
> *And wish for our own sakes, without a Satyr,*
> *You'd less good Breeding, or had more good Nature.*[9]

The Fates were not done with the luckless King's men. Scarcely had the French troupe departed than a band of Italian comedians, led by Tiberio Fiorelli, the famous "Scaramouche" of *commedia dell arte*, arrived fresh from an engagement in Paris. The Italians also acted at York House, and occasionally late in the afternoon at the King's expense in the Whitehall Theatre. At Whitehall only members of the Court, officials, and ladies and gentlemen known to the sentries at the doors were admitted to watch them perform; mere citizens were excluded. From May to September, "Scaramouche" was the talk of the Town.[10]

There seemed to be no end to the misfortunes of the King's Company. For instance, some time in the spring of 1673, a group of titled amateurs, ladies and gentlemen of "Birth & Honour," presented Settle's *The Empress of Morocco* at Whitehall. This was the play's first performance on any stage. In June the Duke's Company produced the play at the Dorset Garden Theatre with all sorts of new scenes and machines. Although the wildly melodramatic story of crime and passion was undoubtedly a great success, it is hardly likely that, as the critic John Dennis wrote later, it "was Acted for a month together." A run of three to six days for a new play was normal; a run of nine to twelve phenomenal.

Ironically, the King's Company should have had this play. Shortly before the Theatre Royal fire, Elkanah Settle, whose first play, *Cambyses*, had been produced by the Duke's Company, carried his second play, *The Empress of Morocco*, to the Theatre Royal. There, he said, "in the height of Mr. Hart's Health and Excellence, I flatter'd my self with the assurance of wonderful success from the performance of so able a company." But, in spite of the fact that on February 27, 1672, Settle was sworn in as "Sewer in Ordinary to His Matie, being one of the poets in His Maties Theatre Royal," it seems that there had been "former Treaties" which bound Settle to offer his work first to the Duke's Company. That company complained to the Duke of York, who decided in favor of his own servants. The decision so enraged Settle that he gave way (he said) to "malignant resentment" against the Duke. Nine years later he took the opportunity "under the umbrage of a popular Champion, to wreak my own private Spight and Revenge"—by libeling York in a political pamphlet, *The Character of a Popish Successor*.[11]

The King's Players, of course, could only nurse their wrongs in silence and do their best with the material at hand, a hastily written propaganda play by over-worked John Dryden. *Amboyna*, a bloody melodrama designed to revive popular interest in the languishing war with Holland, was produced in May or June. It was not a success, but at least it kept the company going.

Very likely Cardell Goodman joined the King's Comedians in the unpropitious spring of 1673, perhaps as a replacement for William Hughes or George Shirley, hirelings who died or resigned about this time. If we assume that Goodman came to London in late November, 1672, we must allow him a month or two to see the sights and spend his small funds on the riotous living to which he quickly became accustomed. He was barely nineteen and, for all his academic learning, he was still a boy from a small town. So far as we know he had no friends in London save crusty Robert Hooke, who lived meanly with his maid, Nell Young, and busied himself with machines and microscopes. After Nell married he lived with his niece, Grace Hooke, who succeeded Nell as his mistress.

For Cardell, alone in a great city, London must have been full of delights: the narrow crowded streets, the shops and stalls piled high with strange wares, the gilded signs, the street cries, the clatter of tongues, and the rumble of drays and coaches. The theatres would attract him, of course, and so would Antonio di Voto, an Italian puppet-master who presented every day in his booth at Charing Cross "variety of Farces, Drolls, and Comical Entertainments." Then there was bear-and-bull baiting at the Beargarden on the Bankside, and sword-fighting at the old Theatre Royal in Vere Street. There was the misty river with its barges, sculls, and ghostly sails; the court at Whitehall with its pageantry of guards in scarlet and black; Westminster Hall, with its booksellers' booths and law courts; the New Exchange in the Strand, where one bought linens and gloves from alluring shop girls; the Tower, with its guns and lions; and, of course, the merry taverns and bawdy houses of Covent Garden. There was no lack of amusement, only of money to pay for it.[12]

Eventually Cardell was accepted by the King's Company as a beginner, or new "hired man." Before 1642, when the theatres were closed by Parliament, a would-be actor enlisted with one of the London companies as a boy, serving as apprentice to a master player. In 1648, when the actors were out of work and starving, a contemporary wrote, "These poore Men were most of them initiated, and bred up in this quality from their Childhood for the service of King and Queen," and could do nothing else. In those earlier days, a boy learned his trade in female roles until his voice cracked within the ring. We are told that, of the original members of the King's Company in 1660, Charles Hart and Walter Clun "were bred up Boys at the Black-friers, and acted Womens Parts. Hart was Robinson's Boy or Apprentice." Similarly "Burt was a Boy first under Shank at the Black-friers, then under Beeston at the Cockpit; and Mohun, and Shatterel were in the same condition with him, at the last place." After 1660, with women playing the roles designed for their sex, there was little need for boys. The companies filled up their ranks with youngsters recommended by patrons and friends of the master players; or with men like Jo Haynes who had served a trial period at one of the nurseries (acting schools) for young actors; or with such players as Anthony Leigh (Duke's) and Philip Griffin (King's), who had started their careers as strollers or unlicensed actors, performing in drolls and interludes at various fairs. We may take it that Cardell was one of those recommended by a friend, perhaps Robert Hooke or Hooke's colleague, Sir Christopher Wren.[13]

It is easy enough to see why he joined the King's Company. Because of its prosperity, the Duke's Company could choose at will among many well-qualified applicants. It had only recently recruited its strength, having lost eight men by death, and three women who "by force of Love were Erept the Stage." It had no opening for an unskilled young gentleman fresh from Cambridge, except, perhaps, as a starveling novice in Lady Davenant's newly organized Nursery in Barbican, outside the northern wall of the old City. But the King's Company was in sore need of hirelings, and, precarious as its condition was in 1673, it engaged a number of promising men, among them Cardell Goodman, Philip Griffin, Carey Perin, Thomas Clarke, John Wiltshire, Nathaniel Kew, John Coysh, a former stroller, and Thomas Sheppey, once a sharing actor in the Duke's Company.[14]

As an apprentice, Cardell had to work a least three months without salary "by Way of Approbation According to Ancient Articles." Even after this trial period, when his pay was fixed at ten to fifteen shillings a week (about as many dollars in modern purchasing power) he still had a long row to hoe before he could be sworn in as a journeyman actor.

Shortly after the beginning of King Charles the Second's reign, it became customary to swear in all the male members of the King's Company—sharing actors, selected hirelings, scenekeepers, book keepers (prompters), doorkeepers, housekeepers, and joiners—as "grooms of the chamber in ordinary without fee." Actresses and female servants—tirewomen and dressmakers—were sworn as "His Maties Weomen Comoedians." The members of the Duke's Company were sworn as "His Royal Highness the Duke of York's Comoedians." As far as I can discover, they had no other titles.

The term "comoedian" was generally used without distinction to describe anyone who worked in the Theatre Royal. For example, Mary Meggs ("Orange Moll"), fruitwoman in the theatre (sworn into office on November 21, 1664), was called a "Comoedian." Henry Hailes, scenekeeper (sworn August 2, 1671), was a "Comoedian in the Theatre." John Bradley, tailor (sworn April 10, 1673), was listed as a "Comoedian in ye Theatre Royall," and even Nathaniel Lee (sworn May 17, 1675) and Thomas D'Urfey (sworn May 8, 1676), poets, were officially "Comoedians or Actors in his Maties Theatre Royall."[15]

As sworn servants of royalty, the actors and servants of both companies came under the authority of the Lord Chamberlain of the Household and could be impressed into the army or navy, or sued or arrested for debt, only with his permission. A properly sworn "comoedian" was eligible for a "protection certificate" from the Lord Chamberlain's office, stating that the bearer was the King's (or the Duke's) servant, and warning "all persons" to forbear arresting or molesting him, "as they will answer the contrary at theire perills."[16]

A special rule seems to have controlled the swearing in of the actors (but not the servants) of the King's Company. At this time the number of sworn actors and actresses was regularly limited by custom to a maximum of sixteen men (shareholders and hirelings) and eleven women, all of whom were entitled to liveries. At the end of every even-numbered year, from 1660 through 1680, the male actors, as grooms of the chamber, were given four yards of bastard scarlet cloth for a livery cloak and a quarter of a yard of crimson velvet for a cape, or cap. But because the male actors had been since January 15, 1662 the "Queenes Maties Comoedians" also, each actually received eight yards of wool and half a yard of velvet. The actresses of the company were granted the larges of single liveries in June, 1666. (The liveries for players cost the King a total of £205 8s 9d every other year). No actor or actress could be properly sworn into the King's service until a vacancy opened among the "sixteene men Comoedians" or the "eleven women Comoedians" already sworn.

Like other apprentices, then, Cardell had to wait for the death, resignation, or discharge of a sworn actor before he could achieve the crimson eminence of a journeyman player. When opportunity offered he could go to Whitehall, armed with a letter from Thomas Killigrew, find out the Lord Chamberlain, the Vice Chamberlain, or any gentleman usher, and take his oath as a groom of the chamber in ordinary without fee, swearing on the Bible to be "a true servant" and to "serve the Kinge truly and ffaythfully," to be "obedient to the Lord Chamberlaine, Vice Chamberlaine, gentlemen ushers, dayly waiters in his Majesty's service," and so forth. Cardell had to wait for three long years.[17]

There were some disadvantages to being one of the King's servants. The Lord Chamberlain could interfere at will in the affairs of either theatre. For various "misdemeanours," such as insubordination, absence from duty, an insult to a noble lord, a quarrel or brawl, or speaking a profane prologue or epilogue, the Lord Chamberlain could send a King's messenger to apprehend the naughty player and could, without a trial, imprison him in the Porter's Lodge at Whitehall or in the Marshalsea. The mildest punishment was a prohibition from acting for awhile, with a consequent loss of income. The most severe was a whipping.

According to John Dennis, "for great Misdemeanours, they [the actors] have been sent to Whitehall, and whipt at the Porter's Lodge. And I have heard Jo. Haines more than once ingenuously own, that he had been whipt twice there." Sometimes the players paid dearly for the dubious honor of being the King's or the Duke's servants.[18]

We know nothing about Goodman's earliest roles, but the chances are that like those of any fledgling they consisted mainly of "walk-on" parts as a soldier, a guard, a servant, or as a faceless member of a crowd. When he was not on-stage or rehearsing, he was learning the techniques of acting. In the chilly tiring room for men—only the master players and one or two leading women had private dressing rooms with fireplaces—he learned how to dress, walk, and talk, and how to use his hands and body in the stylized gestures considered indispensable to good acting. The older players—particularly Hart, Mohun, Wintershall, and Lacy —tutored the hirelings according to their own special skills. One taught them how to use their swords in a stage duel and how to manage a blood-soaked sponge tied to the palm and squeezed against face or body to mimic a wound. Another taught them declamation: how to deliver a "rant," a passage of passionate oratory, without losing breath. One taught them polite manners; another how to sing and how to dance the country dances which so often closed a comedy.

Goodman's private life, too, was probably much like that of his fellows. Because they rehearsed every morning and played every afternoon six days a week, the actors lived as close as possible to the Theatre Royal. Some of the master players had houses in Drury Lane or Russell Street. A favorite location for lodgings, both before the theatre burned down and after it was rebuilt, was Playhouse Yard, a wide entry running from Drury Lane to the theatre. Some of the hirelings found cheap lodgings or boarding houses in Covent Garden or Bloomsbury, and were usually in debt to their landladies.

After their day's work was done, the hirelings were free to haunt the cookshops, taverns, and brothels of Covent Garden, Moorfields, and Whetstone's Park, where they ate, drank, gambled, and roistered, and sometimes ended the night in bed with a night-walker—or an actress. A favorite resort for more sedate actors was the Rose Tavern in Russell Street, where Pepys one memorable night met his fellow-collegian, John Dryden the poet, and Henry Harris, a master player of the Duke's Company, and there was "very witty and pleasant discourse." The sharing players of both companies were well-read, self-educated, hard-working men, who kept regular hours, lived frugally, and went to church on Sundays. But most of the hired men were a swaggering, riotous, lecherous lot, often in trouble with the watch or the Lord Chamberlain for their "severall Misdemeanours." In 1669 Tom Killigrew, Master of the King's Company, told Pepys "that he is fain to keep a woman on purpose at 20s. a week to satisfy 8 or 10 of the young men of his house, whom till he did so he could never keep to their business, and now he do." The story may not have been true—Killigrew was a famous jester—but Pepys and others found it credible enough.[19]

The young women of the playhouses were very little better than the men, and most of them had a weather eye out for a likely "keeper." All the hirelings lived a hand-to-mouth existence, quickly spending their weekly pay, running into debt, cadging from friends, and filching clothes and finery from the playhouse stocks. When the theatres prospered their pay was regular, and there were chances to earn extra money when a company put on a command performance at Whitehall. But sometimes the theatres were closed for a fast day or for Passion Week, for four to six weeks because of the death of an adult member of the royal family, for a month or more in the summer because of the Long Vacation, or indefinitely because of war or plague. At such times the incomes of the sharers stopped too, but since they paid for the theatre only by the acting day and stopped the pay of the hirelings, their overhead was small. The poor hirelings could beg, steal, or starve in the streets.

One could endure much for the hope of applause and pelf. The height of every young player's ambition was to be a sharing actor, or master player. At the King's Theatre there was a weekly accounting around "the sharing table." From the gross income of the theatre Tom Killigrew, the manager, took the lion's share, partly for his own gain but chiefly to pay the company's expenses: rent, wages, pensions, costumes, properties, and the third day's profit of a playwright. The balance was divided among the actor-sharers, who gained in proportion to the company's success. (Those actor-sharers who also owned stock in the theatre building were doubly fortunate.) Since Killigrew had the power to elevate any hireling to the rank of actor-sharer, there was theoretically no limit to a young player's future. However, the eight actor-sharers, who really controlled the company's policies, had no intention of splitting their weekly melon into smaller slices. For the hirelings there was only the rind.

Nevertheless, it was an exciting life, exactly suited to Cardell's tastes and talents. We may take it that he quickly fell into the ways of his fellows and drew heavily upon their knowledge of the Town. The older actors knew most of the regular playgoers by sight and many personally, having met them in the tiring rooms of the theatre or in the galleries of Whitehall Palace. On a good afternoon, with a new play or a popular revival, the players waiting in the scene room could see through a peephole the full pit, with all the beaux in Fop Corner near the stage, and with the side-boxes glorified by beauty and royalty. Such wits as the Duke of Buckingham, the Earl of Rochester, Sir Charles Sedley, Lord Buckhurst, and fat Harry Savile rarely missed the first performance of a new play, even though prices were doubled. On a truly lucky day the King, with toothy little Queen Catherine, would be in his box directly opposite the stage, while the King's brother, long-faced James Duke of York, would be in an adjoining box with his Duchess and a cluster of Maids of Honor. Surely the Duchess of Cleveland would be present, brilliant in blue satin and diamonds, watching the play with heavy-lidded eyes. She was a great theatre-goer, and her latest lover, Will Wycherley, was a successful playwright. Present also might be witty Nell Gwyn and blonde Mary Davis (of whom a "shitten" story was still being told), the two actresses who had helped displace the Duchess of Cleveland as the King's chief mistress. Then, no doubt, the new French mistress, baby-faced Louise Keroualle, Duchess of Portsmouth, would be sitting somewhere near the King. She in her turn had displaced the two actresses, but not completely, of course. The King might discard knaves and jokers from his pack, but never queans.

The actors were quick to hear and repeat all the latest gossip. They could tell Cardell about the Duchess of Cleveland's extravagance: how, only two or three years ago, she had been driven about the streets "with eight horses in her coach, the streets, balconies, and windows full of people to admire her," and how t'other night she had lost a fortune gambling at the Groom Porter's. They knew all the ballads and lampoons about her, and (with a quick look to see that Charles Hart was not nearby) they could repeat the verses made about her when Hart was her lover:

> *Next comes Castlemane*
> *That Prerogative Queene*
> *If I had such a Bitch I would spley her.*
> *She swives like a Stoate*
> *Goes to't Leg & foot*
> *Level coyle with a Prince & a Player.*

Truly Hart was a man to emulate: a rich bachelor with a country house just outside London, with fine clothes and fine women in abundance. If he could be such a success, Cardell, starting with the advantage of a university education could do at least as well—become a sharer and master player, dress in silk and gold lace, aspire to the bed of a duchess, and eat three times a day. Even a hireling could dream.[20]

In July, 1673, the hirelings of the King's Company got a chance to earn double pay for a short time. Frequently in past years the Duke's Company had gone down to Oxford for the university's annual "Act." This was a period of academic jubilation, with lectures, sermons, and a convocation, beginning on the first Monday after July 7. The Duke's Players had profited greatly by presenting two plays a day, morning and afternoon, for ten to twelve days, before mixed audiences of town and gown. Once they reaped a clear profit of £1,500.[21]

Now the King's Company demanded the right to recoup its fortunes with an Oxford venture. On May 12, the Earl of St. Albans, Lord Chamberlain, wrote to the mayor of Oxford, stating his Majesty's pleasure that "His owne servants the Comoedians here should goe down thither for the space of ten days." Of course his Majesty's pleasure was the mayor's command. The

King's Comoedians—master players, hirelings, scenekeepers, and doormen—with trunks full of clothes and properties, journeyed down to Oxford by coach. On July 14 they set up their stage in a tennis court, and thereafter succeeded as they had wished.

For one play at Oxford, Jonson's *The Silent Woman,* Dryden wrote a prologue and an epilogue which were fulsome in their praise of the halls of Academe. He sent copies to his friend, John Wilmot, Earl of Rochester. "Your Lordship," he wrote, "will judge how easy 'tis to pass any thing upon an University; and how grosse flattery the learned will endure." In his epilogue Dryden listed the company's recent troubles in London. "A French Troop," too quick and hot to stay, had left behind an itch for novelty, and a troupe of "Italian Merry-Andrews" (Fiorelli's players) had succeeded them:

> *Stout Scaramoucha with Rush Lance rode in,*
> *And ran a Tilt at Centaure Arlequin.*
> *For Love you heard how amorous Asses bray'd,*
> *And Cats in Gutters gave their Serenade.*
> *Nature was out of Countenance, and each Day*
> *Some new born Monster shewn you for a Play.*

Then, "to strike the Stage quite Dumb," the Duke's House with its French machines and its operatic *Macbeth* had put Fletcher and Jonson quite out of fashion and had left "Wit the onely Drug in all the Nation." Dryden's ire rose as his profits sank.[22]

In the running war between the theatres it was time for the King's Comoedians to take the offensive. When they returned to London in late July, Thomas Duffett (dramatist, poetaster, and once a milliner in the New Exchange) hurriedly dashed off for them a travesty of Settle's popular *The Empress of Morocco.* Following the pattern set by Buckingham's *The Rehearsal* (still one of the more popular plays in the King's Company's repertory), Duffett trimmed kings and heroes down to corn-cutters, draymen, porters, tapsters, and chimney sweeps. Completely plotless and written in bad hudibrastic verse, Duffett's *Empress of Morocco* is good fun but worthless as drama. Evidently the master players thought it beneath their dignity and turned it over to the hired men as a "vacation play or an after-piece," giving Cardell Goodman what was probably his first chance to create a role.

All the characters were acted by men in blackface. The Old Empress in Settle's play became a bawd, played by Will Harris. Princess Mariamne became a cinder-wench (Goodman), and the young Empress Morena became an apple-woman (Philip Griffin). Only one of the hirelings, Marmaduke Watson, who played "Crimalhaz a Strong-water-man," was an old, experienced actor; the rest were young men, and three of them—Kempton, Venner, and Adams—were novices who are never heard of again.[23]

To lengthen the production and to fire another shot at the Duke's House, Duffett added a lengthy epilogue, "Being a new Fancy after the Old, and most surprising way of Macbeth." This was a complete skit in itself, with songs and spirits and "Cats and Musicians," with witches flying over the pit "Riding upon Beesoms"; with Heccate (Martin Powell) descending to the stage in a chariot "made of a large Wicker Basket," and with men dressed as Thunder (Goodman) and Lightning (Kew) "discover'd, not behind Painted Tiffany to blind and amuse the Senses, but openly by the most excellent way of Mustard-bowl and Salt-Peter." (That is, on the open stage Thunder pounded on a large wooden bowl and Lightning flashed pans of gunpowder.) The best of the songs, sung to a popular tune, proposed the health of five famous bawds: Mother Cresswell, Madam Gifford, Sister Temple, Betty Buley, and Mother Moseley. As Mariamne, Goodman had only three short speeches to memorize, and as Thunder in the epilogue he had nothing at all to say. At least his name appeared for the first time in the dramatis personae of a printed play.

The withers of the Duke's Players were unwrung. "Having then plenty of poets" and the pick of the new plays, they went their prosperous way. In September they countered with Arrowsmith's comedy *The Reformation,* in which the character of the know-it-all Tutor, clearly a personal attack on Dryden, may have been written in revenge for Dryden's savage prologues and epilogues. In the autumn neither company had a new play to offer, but the Duke's Company was well supplied with successes, including Pordage's bombastic melodrama, *Herod and Mariamne,* first produced about 1671. Of this play, the story is that Pordage, seeking the Earl of Rochester's patronage (and perhaps an introduction to the King's Company), had left the manuscript for

THE KING'S COMPANY   31

his perusal. A week later he had returned to find his play "in the Hands of the Porter, with this Distich wrote upon the cover of it:

> *Poet who e'er thou art, God damn thee,*
> *Go hang thyself, and burn thy Mariamne."*

But Rochester was an intellectual and a wit; the audiences thronging to the Dorset Garden theatre were not so captious. With revivals of *Herod and Mariamne, Sir Martin Mar-all, Epsom Wells,* and *The Empress of Morocco,* the Duke's Players ended the year in triumph.[24]

But there were renewed hopes for the King's Company. On December 17, 1673, the master players signed a final agreement with the builders of the new theatre, now nearly finished, binding themselves to pay £3 10s for every acting day. Early in the next year the company, desperate for new plays, presented in succession two foolish comedies, Dover's *The Mall* and "a Person of Honour's" *The Amorous Old Woman,* both of which failed, perhaps because the master players were so busy with their new house that they left most of the playing to the inexperienced hirelings. Once again hard-working John Dryden saved the day with an old comedy warmed over, and with a new scene added in his own hand. *The Mistaken Husband,* the last new play presented at the old Lincoln's Inn Fields tennis court, was produced in late February or early March. The epilogue, spoken by a woman, held out promises of "a fine House, and Clothes a making."[25]

The new Theatre Royal, built on the site of the old, was probably constructed after designs by Sir Christopher Wren, with the usual sloping pit, side-boxes, and two rows of galleries. The oval stage, where most of the action took place, jutted well out into the pit before the proscenium. There were two entrances on each side. The stage was lighted by chandeliers and footlights, and the house by six windows on each side. The inner stage was equipped with sliding scenes which opened or closed to "discover" a new setting. Of course there was the usual complement of trapdoors through which actors could rise or disappear, and of simple machines to pull singers, scenes, or tables up into the heavens, or to move them about the stage. The theatre building cost nearly £4,000. An adjoining scene house cost £2,040, a sum raised by contributions from the master players, ranging from £160 to £200 each.[26]

The theatre opened on March 26, 1674, with a revival of Brome's *The Beggars Bush*. In a prologue written for the occasion Dryden was careful to explain why the King's Company could offer only "A Plain Built House after so long a stay." Not only was this the best the company could afford, but "Our Royal Master will'd it should be so." The King's Comedians begged only for permission to live; they could not hope to vie with their "Great Neighbours," the Duke's Company,

> *Who build and Treat with such Magnificence;*
> *That like th'Ambitious Monarchs of the Age,*
> *They give the Law to our Provincial Stage.*

Besides, there was no sense in building "a stately Pile"

> *Whilst Scenes, Machines, and empty Opera's reign,*
> *And for the Pencil You the Pen disdain.*
> *While Troops of famisht Frenchmen hither drive,*
> *And laugh at those upon whose Alms they live.*

Evidently Dryden had heard (as who had not?) of the preparations for a magnificent operatic version of *The Tempest* at the Duke's House, and he concluded wryly,

> *I wou'd not prophesie our Houses Fate:*
> *But while vain Shows and Scenes you over-rate,*
> *'Tis to be fear'd—*
> *That as a Fire the former House o'rethrew,*
> *Machines and Tempests will destroy the new.*

The speaker, Hart or Mohun, bowed, stepped back, and the play began. The Theatre Royal was in business again.[27]

III

The War of the Theatres

For the next three years after the opening of the new Theatre Royal all we know about Cardell Goodman is that on November 20, 1674, he borrowed twenty shillings from Robert Hooke and that on June 8, 1676, he was sworn in as a member of the King's Company, "a groom of the great Chamber in ordinary without fee." His obscurity is not surprising. Despite their pretense to gentility, players were people of no importance, rating with butchers, carpenters, drapers, and shoemakers. Even in the lists of the King's servants they came last, after the huntsmen, watermen, and the royal ratkiller. Offstage they were rarely noticed; they kept no diaries, and few of their letters were preserved. Such virtuosos of biography as John Aubrey and Anthony Wood devoted pages to bilious bishops, trifling poets, and pip-squeak lords, and had hardly a word to say about the greatest actors of their time.[1]

The name of a Restoration actor must be sought for in the dramatis personae of printed plays; or in church records of births, marriages, and funerals; or in legal records of accusations, true bills, convictions, and chancery suits; or in the Lord Chamberlain's lists of the King's servants, petitions for the right to sue, and warrants for appointments, liveries, or arrests for misdemeanors. From his arrival in London until January, 1677, Cardell was officially noticed only in the Lord Chamberlain's records and in the dramatis personae of Duffett's *Empress of Morocco*. According to the negative evidence, then, he paid his debts, learned his trade, and committed neither matrimony nor murder. He seems to have had affairs with a series of amiable young women, but, being a gentleman, he kept quiet about them.

It is not surprising that his name appeared in the dramatis personae of only one play. So far as we know, in the years 1674, 75, and 76 the King's Company produced only seventeen new plays, operas, burlesques, or revivals worth printing. (The Duke's Company produced twenty-four.) Of those seventeen only ten include the names of the players who acted roles of importance. Pure chance, or the whim of the author, or of the bookseller who had the play printed, dictated whether any actors' names should appear in the dramatis personae, and if so, whose. In one play we have the names of twelve actors (five sharers and seven hirelings) and five actresses; in another, with a cast calling for ten men and four women, we are given the names of the actresses, but of only four actors, all shareholders. It follows, then, that for all we know Goodman may have played some minor part—a soldier, messenger, priest, senator, or what-not—in every new play, and he surely must have played dozens of lesser roles in revivals of stock plays.

It is very unlikely that he created a leading role in a new play during those three years. Although Charles Hart, the company's leading man, was in failing health, he seems to have clung tenaciously to his rights, allowing no one to substitute for him in a new play. It is tempting to suggest that tall, handsome Cardell, a potential leading man who eventually inherited the older actor's roles, was Hart's understudy, but small repertory companies could not afford spares. Every man who had a part in a play was expected to keep his lines in memory, and to play the role again at a revival with perhaps no more than a day's notice. If a leading actor fell sick, either the announced play was cancelled and another substituted or another actor was hastily rehearsed in the part.

Presumably, after a year or two of study Cardell became a competent enough actor, but in the pecking order of the green room he was barely inside the door. Ahead of him in the competition for parts when he joined the company were three highly competent hirelings with from eight to twelve years' experience —Marmaduke Watson, Thomas Hancock, and Edward Lydall—

and four men with from three to five years' experience—Jo Haynes, William Harris, Martin Powell (an ex-stroller), and George Beeston (who disappeared about 1675). Most of his immediate contemporaries outranked him and were sworn in as members of the company before he was: Clarke *ca.* September, 1674, Griffin and Coysh on November 9, 1674, Sheppey on January 15, 1675, and Wiltshire on May 22, 1675. Of course lesser hirelings appeared from time to time, players too transient to mention, who left their names on the records but no footprints on the stage. Of all the train of fit and unfit at this time, only Goodman, Powell, Coysh, Griffin, Clarke, and Wiltshire grew into accomplished and useful actors—and the best of these was Goodman.[2]

But Cardell's fame was yet to come. In the meantime he lived the spare, penurious life of a typical hireling, with never quite enough to eat, and with his clothes "bare worn." From Colley Cibber's erratic memory of Goodman reminiscences in 1696 we can draw one anecdote of these early days. Goodman and Philip Griffin (says Colley) "were confined by their moderate Sallaries to the Œconomy of lying together in the same Bed and having but one whole Shirt between them: One of them being under the obligation of a Rendezvous with a fair Lady, insisted on his wearing it out of his Turn, which occasion'd so high a dispute that the Combat was immediately demanded, and accordingly their Pretensions to it were decided by a fair Tilt upon the spot, in the Room where they lay: But whether Clytus [Griffin] or Alexander [Goodman] was obliged to see no Company till a worse [shirt] could be wash'd for him, seems not to be a material point in their History."[3]

Ill-paid though he was, shirtless Cardell had no recourse except to give up the theatre. He could earn no more at the Duke's Theatre or at the Smock Alley Theatre in Dublin; anyway he could not join another troupe without a certificate of discharge from the King's Company. Even in periods when the theatres were closed, he was subject to arrest and punishment if he clubbed with other unlicensed comedians to present "interludes and stage plays" elsewhere in London, and if he joined some vagrant strolling troupe in the provinces he would lead an even more beggarly existence. There is no doubt that every hireling suffered for his art, especially in the Long Vacation when (as the famous stroller Tony Aston said), "Harlots, Poets, and Players are all poor." But the hope of applause, of getting a fat part, of eventually displacing some aged actor and becoming a master player kept every hireling alive. Like an understudy of modern days he dogged the lead's life, praying for him to drop dead, or at least fall sick. We are told that once when Buckingham's *The Rehearsal* was to be revived, "The Famous Lacy, whose part was that of Bays, unseasonably falls sick of the Gout. . . . Haynes is looked upon as the fittest Person to supply the place of the Distempered, His Grace [of Buckingham] himself being pleased to instruct him in the Nature of the Part. . . . So well did Haynes perform it, that the Earl of R[ochester] Lord B[uckhurst] Sir Charles S[edley] and several of the most Ingenious men, ever after held him in high esteem." Considering the ages and ailments of the master players, the hirelings of the King's Company must have lived from day to day on the tip-toe of expectancy.[3]

Goodman had no such luck as Haynes. We look in vain for the dramatic episode in his stage career, when he substituted for a master player and covered himself with glory. From 1673 to 1677 he was an undistinguished hireling, and his life story is that of the King's Company. In the never-ending war of the theatres he shared in every victory or defeat. Since the losses far outnumbered the gains, he must have been a young man of sanguine temperament and endless patience.

Because their new theatre was located in Covent Garden close to the mansions and lodgings of their patrons, the King's players should have prospered. The war with Holland had ended on February 19, 1674; the warrior-wits had returned to their wonted amusements; and the gentry had come back to Town from their country estates. But the players suffered from internal quarrels and lack of leadership. Tom Killigrew was a famous wit, an accomplished courtier, a passable playwright, and a wretched theatrical manager. His personal finances were so tangled as to baffle accountants, and the affairs of the Theatre Royal were in little better shape. Moreover, because of the limitations of their theatre, the King's Company could not easily satisfy the new popular taste for operas, those curious hybrids of drama, music, songs, dances, painted scenes, and elaborate machines, which the Duke's Company had already catered to with its musical version of *Macbeth*. Obliged to offer a steady diet of solid drama, the Theatre Royal appealed only to the sensible and sober, while the Dorset Garden Theatre drew the feather-brained mobs—then, as always, in the majority.

In April, 1674, after a long period of preparation and rehearsal, the Duke's Players produced an operatic version of *The Tempest*, as altered first by Davenant and Dryden, and second by Thomas Shadwell. To mount it sumptuously they bought new scenes and intricate imported machines, hired singers from the Royal Chapel and French dancers led by the famous St. André, and commissioned music by Draghi, Matthew Locke, Pietro Reggio, and James Hart. In the prologue and epilogue to the opera the Duke's Comedians flung defiance in the envious teeth of the "reverend" King's Players, accused them of penny-pinching, and bragged of their own lavish prodigality to please their customers:

> *We have machines to some perfection brought,*
> *And above 30 warbling voyces gott.*
> *Many a God & Goddesse you will heare,*
> *And we have Singing, Dancing, Devills here,*
> *Such Devills, and such gods, are very Deare.*
> *We, in all ornaments, are lavish growne,*
> *And like Improvident Damsells of ye Towne,*
> *For present bravery, all our wealth lay downe.*

It was wealth well invested. Because of the throngs of spectators and the fact that prices were doubled for all performances (not merely the first, as usual), "not any succeeding Opera got more Money." The initial run lasted at least two weeks, but the Town continued to call for revivals. The opera was presented again in June, when Robert Hooke saw it; in September, when Nell Gwyn saw it three times; and in November, when the King saw it twice. *The Tempest* became a stock opera, sure of a profitable run whenever it was presented.[4]

Against such a sweeping success (plus, for good measure, new plays by Crowne, Payne, Settle, and the Duke of Newcastle) the unhappy King's Company could set as its major attractions for the year only a poor attempt at a French opera, *Ariane, ou le Mariage de Bacchus*, "Acted by the Royal Academy of Musick" in March, and Lee's "bloody, fatal play," *The Tragedy of Nero*, in May. They were not enough to stem the tide; playgoers continued to flock to the Dorset Garden Theatre in spite of its inconvenient location in the City.

In July, hoping for another profitable tour, the King's Company journeyed down to Oxford again for the Act. This time they were ill received, "not haveing gained so much as after all things payed to make a dividend of £10 to the chiefe sharers." Disappointed by their reception, the swashbuckling youngsters of the company—Goodman, Griffin, Coysh, Wiltshire, and their friends—were guilty of "great rudenesses . . . going about the town in the night breaking of windows, and committing many other unpardonable rudenesses"—evidently too vulgar for description. Their misbehavior cost the company the right to return the next year.[5]

Back in London, the King's Players turned again to Thomas Duffett, who wrote for them a full length travesty called *The Mock-Tempest: Or, The Enchanted Castle*, probably produced in August by "the young people"—the hirelings—for their own benefit. Duffett turned Shakespeare's magic island into Bridewell Prison, presided over by the farceur Jo Haynes as Duke Prospero. Dainty little Ariel was played by Betty Mackarel, a big, handsome orange-girl, famed for wit and wantonness—truly a tricksy spirit. No other actors' names are given, but the chances are that Goodman had a part. Prospero's daughters Miranda and Dorinda (a character added in the altered versions) became silly, sex-hungry wenches; Prince Ferdinand became a religious nonconformist named Quakero; and Stephano, the butler, turned into Stephania, a bawdy house matron with an entourage of Bridewell whores, Beantosser, Moustrappa, and Drinkallup. Probably all four roles were played by men. A fair sample of the play's outrageous humor is the parody of Ariel's song in V, 1, of the original, sung by gigantic Betty Mackarel:

> *Where good Ale is, there suck I,*
> *In a Coblers Stall I lye,*
> *While the Watch are passing by;*
> *Then about the Streets I fly,*

> *After Cullies merrily.*
> *And I merrily, merrily take up my clo'se,*
> *Under the Watch, and the Constables Nose.*

There is no reason to believe that the burlesque version had any effect at all on the success of the opera, but *The Mock-Tempest* was at least popular enough to be revived in November, coincidentally with a revival of *The Tempest*. King Charles, who liked his comedy broad and coarse, saw it at the Theatre Royal on November 19.[6]

Still burdened by debts and troubled by quarrels with their manager, at the beginning of 1675 the master players got together with Tom Killigrew under the friendly eye of the Lord Chamberlain and agreed that thenceforth "halfe of ye profit of the House shall goe towards the paymt of ye Debts of ye House." The effect of the agreement was to cut in half the incomes of the shareholders and to make sure that no hireling could hope for a raise. Almost immediately thereafter, in spite of diminished morale, the company scored a success with a new comedy, *The Country Wife*, by William Wycherley, who had shifted his loyalty again. A comedy of sex intrigue, *The Country Wife* was so bawdy as to shock even some of the ultra-sophisticates in the audience, but at least everybody had to see it. Five master players, Hart, Kynaston, Mohun, Cartwright, and Shatterel, played the major roles, with Lydall as Dorilant, Haynes as Sparkish (a part designed, probably, for Lacy), and a bevy of beauties for the feminine roles, including Betty Boutell, Elizabeth James, and Elizabeth Knepp.[7]

Their triumph was short-lived. On February 27 the Duke's Players produced their third spectacular opera, *Psyche*, written by Thomas Shadwell, with dances by St. André, music by Locke and Draghi, and scenes by the painter Stevenson. Costing £800 to mount, it was almost twice as expensive as *The Tempest*. It ran for "about 8 days together" at double prices and was frequently revived thereafter. Yet, as John Downes, prompter of the Duke's Company, pointed out, "the Tempest got more money," and malicious Elkanah Settle wrote later, "I have often heard the Players cursing at their oversight in laying out so much on so misliked a Play . . . and that for the future they expect the *Tempest*, which cost not one third of *Psyche*, will be in request when the other is forgotten." Because Settle was venting his spleen against Shadwell, we must discount his gossip. Certainly the opera was successful enough to take away the audiences from the Theatre Royal.[8]

Gambling on dubious new plays, the King's Company produced three during Easter and Trinity terms: Lee's *Sophonisba*, Belon's *The Mock-Duellist*, and Fane's *Love in the Dark*. None could compete with the offerings at the Dorset Garden Theatre. In June came another blow below the belt. During the previous autumn, York House with its old-fashioned theatre had been torn down to make room for new streets and private mansions. But King Charles wanted to see Fiorelli's Italian players again, and there was no theatre available in all London. Therefore, ignoring the monopoly he had granted the two public theatres in 1661, the faithless monarch offered Scaramouche the Hall Theatre in Whitehall Palace, with the right to charge admission "as at a common Playhouse." He even ordered a twelve-penny gallery built "for the convenience of his Majesty's poorer subjects." Decent people were scandalized at the debasing of a theatre built for royal recreation, and the players, of course, were furious. A news writer predicted the obvious: that the arrangement would "half break both our houses."[9]

In spite of murmurs and complaints, the Italians played at Whitehall until late September. It seems that as a concession to the patentees they began their daily performances at five o'clock in the evening, when the plays at the public theatres were over. Although both patent houses suffered, it is possible that the Duke's House suffered more. It had placed its reliance on spectacle and opera, and the Italians were experts at both. Moreover, because of its location in the City, the Duke's House drew a good part of its audience thence. Now, for a mere shilling, any ordinary citizen could get into the King's private theatre, a place usually closed to him.[10]

The King's Players kept up the fight during the summer of 1675, but there is reason to think that the Duke's Theatre simply closed for the Long Vacation. Duffett, in his prologue to a revival of *Everyman Out of His Humour* at the King's House in July railed at the Italians as the "drolling stroling Royal Troop" at Whitehall. In his epilogue he pointed out,

> *How crosly and how kindly things do go!*
> *Though forreign troop does very pow'rful grow,*
> *Kind Justice beats down our domestick foe.*
> *Th'inchanted Castle is once more overthrown,* [The Duke's
> *That Nursery where all the youth in town*
> *Such deeds of Valour and of Love have shown.*
> *Britain's Low Countreys, where at mighty rates*
> *The younger Brothers urg'd their needy Fates,*
> *And th'Elder got diseases for Estates.*[11]

In August the "young people" of the King's Company produced another of Duffett's travesties, *Psyche Debauch'd*. It was getting to be a habit: every spring the Duke's Company produced a new opera, and every summer the King's Company burlesqued it. Introduced by a prologue in which the King's Players solemnly paid tribute to the best actors of the opposition company,

> *That is, the Painter, Carpenter, and show,*
> *Beaumont and Fletcher, Poet, and Devow* [de Voto],

the parody followed familiar lines. Psyche, beloved by Cupid, became None-so-fair, played in petticoats by craggy-faced Jo Haynes. Cupid became "Bruine, the White Bear of Norwich," acted by Will Harris, in furs. None-so-fair's suitors, Prince Nicholas and Prince Philip, were played by little Mrs. Knepp (in breeches), and Peter Charlton, a boy. Goodman's name is missing from the dramatis personae, although Lydall, Coysh, Powell, Wiltshire, and Clarke all had supporting roles. The plot, a tissue of nonsense, concluded with Bruine's admission that he was really "Deval," the famous highwayman. (Claude Duval was executed at Tyburn on January 21, 1670, but his memory lingered on.) It was all a lot of foolishness, "grand foppery," as Robert Hooke called it when he saw the burlesque August 27.[12]

This time the Duke's Company retorted in kind. Toward the end of the Long Vacation the women of the company put on an anonymous tragedy, *Piso's Conspiracy*, playing both the male and female roles. The prologue references to play-bills "in Praise o'th' Beauty of Miss-Non-so-Fair" and to the fact that

> Our Men Players are out of Heart
> Of being seen in a Heroic Part:
> What with Prince Nick, and t'other House Gallants,
> They have run Hero's out of Countenance,

suggest that the Duke's Company was hurt by the slings and arrows of outrageous parody. But *Piso's Conspiracy* was a poor and empty play, however alluring the legs of the actresses in breeches.

Score one for the Theatre Royal, and score again in the autumn, when the Duke's House produced only Otway's mediocre *Alcibiades*, while the King's Company took the Town with one of Dryden's best tragedies, *Aurenge-Zebe*. Yet as Dryden pointed out in the prologue to his play,

> We and our Neighbours, to speak proudly, are
> Like Monarchs, ruin'd with expensive War.

His complaint certainly applied to the King's Company. All that year profits had run so far short of expectation that several times Hart, Wintershall, Kynaston, and Cartwright had given Tom Killigrew notice that "they were minded to give over and desist from acting." The Duke's Company, too, while much better off than its rival, had its financial problems. The fact is that the theatrical hey-day of the sixties was over. Plays were no longer novelties; the best plays of the old masters had become shopworn by frequent repetition; many of the new plays were sheer rubbish; and the audiences, largely composed of gentry, were turning to other forms of entertainment: balls, dances, picnics, masquerades, and music meetings.[13]

Well led, the King's Company might have survived, but Killigrew had lost all control, and his company was slowly disintegrating. In December, 1675, the eight master players got together with him and drew up a set of rules "for the Better Regulateing theire Maties Servants the Comedians at the Royall Theatre." From these it is clear that hirelings were carelessly throwing away their handwritten "parts," refusing to play the roles assigned to them, neglecting rehearsals, taking clothes, feathers, and properties out of the theatre, and pressing in disorderly mobs about the "shareing Table" on pay days. Even the orange-girls in the pit were annoying actors and audience with their noise, in addition to "offending them in the pit" by "treading upon theire Cloathes." Although violators could be fined as much as a week's wages, the abuses continued.[14]

In January, 1676, the company pulled itself together long enough to put on a fine performance of Lee's new tragedy, *Gloriana*, with Charles Hart as the hero, of course. The epilogue, spoken by Haynes, repeated what was becoming a litany for both theatres:

> *But Sirs, what makes it now so hard I pray*
> *To get you here but just at a New Play?*
> *We've Play'd t'oblige you all that's in our pow'rs,*
> *We've Play'd and Play'd our selves e'en out of doors,*
> *And yet we cannot find one way to win ye;*
> *You've grown so nice, I think the Devil's in ye.*

Haynes concluded by suggesting flagellation as a means of stimulating jaded theatrical appetites.

In February dissension erupted again, and finally the eight master players simply quit. On February 14, the King, taking notice of their "private differences & disagreemts," sternly ordered them back to work again. Very likely his first command was ignored; ten days later the Lord Chamberlain ordered the master players arrested and brought before him "to answer such things as shall be objected against them." Peace was patched up for the moment, and on May 1 Charles Killigrew, with the approval of Thomas, his father, persuaded the actors to enter into a new agreement with him as their manager. Then Thomas went back on his promise to turn the reins over to Charles, and war broke out again between actors and managers, and father and son. In August the King ordered the Theatre Royal closed until the dust settled, and in September the Lord Chamberlain appointed Hart, Mohun, Kynaston, and Cartwright a committee to manage the company's affairs. Later he appointed Hart to act alone.[15]

At the height of this battle-royal, on June 8, 1676, Cardell Goodman was sworn in as a comedian, a groom of the chamber without fee, replacing Thomas Hancock, who had given up either the game or the ghost. Cardell was twenty-two years old. Three years after entering the company he had reached the second rung on the ladder of success, and he could wear his scarlet livery cloak with pride. But he was still a hireling, with small reputation or prestige in the company, and his salary was probably no more than thirty shillings a week.[16]

The King's Company produced three more new plays in 1676, D'Urfey's *The Siege of Memphis* in September, his *The Fool Turn'd Critick* in November, and Wycherley's *The Plain Dealer* in December. For daily fare it warmed up old plays, in one of which Cardell Goodman may have had an important part. On December 4, 1676, King Charles saw a performance of *Julius Caesar* at the Theatre Royal. In a production of this play *ca.* 1671–72 the major roles, Brutus, Cassius, and Mark Antony, were played by Hart, Mohun, and Kynaston, while Caesar was played by Richard Bell, the young hireling who was blown up in the Theatre Royal fire. An edition of *Julius Caesar* printed in 1684 has a United Company cast with Kynaston as Antony and Goodman as Caesar (Hart died in 1682, Mohun in 1684). Since it was customary to assign roles in revivals to actors who had played them before, it is at least likely that Goodman played Caesar in the revival of 1676.[17]

Frequently upset by quarrels and closures, the King's Company had very thin profits in 1676. The peaceful Duke's Company played on steadily, producing no new operas but eleven new plays, most of them successes. We know, for example, that Thomas D'Urfey

> *had the Honour to Tickle*
> *The Ears of the Town with his dear Madam Fickle,*

that Shadwell's *The Virtuoso* (which libelled Robert Hooke) "got the Company great Reputation," Otway's *Titus and Berenice* "had good Success," Etherege's *The Man of Mode* "being well Cloath'd and well Acted, got a great deal of Money," and Otway's *Don Carlos* "lasted successively 10 Days; it got more money than any preceding Modern Tragedy." The Duke's Comedians were not rolling in wealth, but at least most of them were solvent.[18]

The unhappy condition of the King's Company in the years 1673–77 is illustrated by a number of petitions to the Lord Chamberlain for permission to sue the company or its employees—hirelings, scenekeepers, and joiners—for debt. For example, on February 26, 1673, William Hughes was petitioned against for a debt of £10, and on March 14, Edward Eastland, book keeper, owed "£8 or thereabouts." On October 25, Henry Wright, scenekeeper, was sued for an unspecified sum. On June 3, 1674, it appears that Eastland's debt, now £10, was still unpaid. On September 4, Jo Haynes was petitioned against for a debt of £4, and on November 18, for £15. On February 6, 1675, Robert Shatterel (as agent for the company) was charged with a debt of £500. On February 10, we have Haynes again for £24 "for dyet and Lodgings." On June 15, "Mr. Wintersell and the rest of the Comoedians" were petitioned against for a debt of £90. On June 30, Haynes was summoned by the Lord Chamberlain to explain what he was going to do about a debt of £10, and on December 22, for an unpaid bond of £30. Poor Haynes started the list for 1676 with a new debt of £7, and Martin Powell joined him quickly with a debt of £5, followed in March by a joint debt of £5 with John Coysh. Cardell Goodman's debt of £3 for "money lent" in January, 1677, was a trifle in comparison with the company's debts of £34 and £135 in May "for goods sold and delivered." These, of course, were merely the cases presented to the Lord Chamberlain by long-suffering creditors. It is unlikely that any of the hirelings of the King's Company was completely solvent during these years, and the company itself was falling ever deeper into debt. The Lord Chamberlain did his best to head off law suits against the hirelings, usually ordering an offender to pay his creditor a few shillings a week, "every weeke he shall act at his Mats Theatre," until the debt was paid. Thus on January 22, 1677, he ordered Goodman to pay Thomas Kite, a tradesman in Angel Court, Longacre, three shillings a week for twenty weeks. If Cardell failed to keep up his payments, Mr. Kite could get permission to sue the unfortunate player, arrest him, and throw him into debtors' prison.[19]

One may well wonder how the poor hirelings managed to survive. When the King's Company was inactive during the Long Vacation the young people scraped along like grasshoppers in the sun. If the shareholders permitted them to play for their own benefit, they did very well. Otherwise, the women had to fall back on husbands, lovers, or families, and the men had to go a-strolling to Cambridge, Norwich, or to Newmarket when the King and his Court were there for the races. Others found jobs acting in booths in Bartholomew Fair in late August and early September, presenting drolls and farces. Once Martin Powell and John Coysh took a vacation job coaching the Duchess of Portsmouth's household servants, who played Dryden's *Indian Emperor* before their mistress and her guests. To stiffen the amateurs, Powell played Montezuma and Coysh acted Cortez. If we can believe some of the stories about Jo Haynes, in vacation periods that fantastic player went from the sublime to the ridiculous as a stroller, a confidence man, a fortune teller, a quack doctor, a dancing master, an attorney and a nonconformist preacher![20]

Haynes was a rogue by nature; other players became rogues because of their poverty and the temptations of their world. During the theatrical season the poorly paid hirelings in their shabby clothes daily saw and envied people of wealth—sophisticated ladies and rakehell gallants, well fed, richly dressed, and glittering with jewels. Tempted to emulate their betters, some hirelings fell into ungodly ways. An actress invited to sup with a gallant would slip out after the play wearing the theatre's "French gown a-la-mode" in which she had appeared on the stage. Afterward it was easier to sell it than to restore it to its proper place. To impress a coy countess, an actor would steal an expensive plume or a pair of embroidered gloves. From playhouse pilfering to petty theft at large was an easy step. When the theatres were closed a few desperate hirelings turned to strong-arm methods. In 1702, when the theatres were silenced after King William's death, it was reported that "none will suffer by the King's death but the poor players who are ready to starve. . . . One cannot pass by the Play-house now when it is dark but you are sure to be stripped."[21]

A few hirelings went on to even more daring crimes. A favorite occupation of the small criminal was "clipping" coins—trimming off the edges of broad money with a pair of shears and filing the coins smooth. Usually a clipper sold the resultant silver to shady silversmiths. Bolder men melted the clippings and stamped out their own coins. The penalty for either clipping or coining was the same as for high treason: drawing, hanging, and quartering for a man, burning at the stake for a woman.

There is no way of knowing how many hirelings played this little game; but occasionally one was caught and convicted. In September, 1693, Thomas Percival, a long-time member of the Duke's Company, was accused of clipping. Pursued by officers, he dropped a pair of shears and a file. The bailiffs found a small bag of clippings in his pocket and another bagful in his lodgings. Percival's claim that he had found the tools and clippings in a closet in his lodgings and was on his way to take them to a justice was not allowed, and he was condemned to death. In response to pleadings by his daughter, the popular comedienne Susanna Mountfort, Queen Mary commuted his sentence to transportation, but he died on the way to Portsmouth. Matthew Coppinger, a comedian, a strolling player, and something of a poet, had a worse fate. "A notorious clipper," he impersonated an officer and under pretense of searching for clippers, "robbed many houses." On February 28, 1695, he was prosaically hanged at Tyburn. Cardell Goodman was luckier. Although it was well known that he was "concerned with clippers," he was never caught.[22]

Highwaymen were the aristocrats of the underworld. Anyone who "took to the road" knew that the chances were ten to one he would end his life on the gallows at Tyburn, but the severity of the punishment was no deterrent. Single operators and bands of robbers infested the roads of seventeenth-century England, even to the outskirts of London. The solitary rider plodding through a muddy lane never knew when a horseman would loom suddenly out of the mist, whip out a brace of pistols, and cry, "Stand and deliver!" Hated by the rich, loved by the poor, and idolized by brainless youth, some highwaymen became legends. Journalists and ballad singers celebrated their romantic lives, and booksellers published their dying confessions to edify the godly. The ideal highwaymen—Claude Duval, Captain James Hind, Captain Dick Dudley, and William Davis "the Golden Farmer" —were gentlemen who robbed with grace, killed with regret, and repented not at all.

At least two members of the King's Company, Thomas Clarke

and Cardell Goodman, turned their talents to robbery. In July, 1677, a highwayman, John Hodges, caught in the act and lodged in Hertford Jail, turned King's evidence in the hope of a pardon. In his confession he declared that "Clarke, a player belonging to the king's playhouse lodged att a Joyners in Drury Lane, sett York Coach"—that is, acted as "finger-man"—for a band of four robbers who held up the coach and got away with £100. So far as I can discover, no formal charge was ever made against Thomas Clarke.[23]

In the spring of 1681, Cardell Goodman was charged with highway robbery. No record of his trial has been found, but a warrant for the King's pardon is extant. There can be no doubt about his guilt. In 1696 he bragged to Cibber about his adventurous youth, made light of his follies, and claimed that he took to the road because he was so poorly paid. At a guess, then, he began his career by moonlight sometime between 1676 and 1680, when the King's Company was at its nadir, and the actors were living on credit stretched thin. More adventurous than Clarke, Cardell never joined a gang. Instead he seems to have performed in solitary splendor, but sometimes he had the help of a friend, William O'Brian, a corporal in the Earl of Oxford's regiment of horse.[24]

An entry in the Lord Chamberlain's records for March 20, 1677, is an entrancing subject for speculation. On that date one John Lane, who lived "nere ye 3 horses in Hart street Covent Garden," demanded payment "for a mare hyred & spoyled by Goodman worth above six pounds." Was the mare "spoyled" by hard riding when Goodman fled from the hue-and-cry through the thundering night? History is silent, but the prosaic Lord Chamberlain, valuing the ruined mare at only five pounds, ordered Cardell to give John Lane four shillings a week ("dureing such tyme as his Mats Company of Comoedians shall act") until it was paid for.[25]

IV

The Lean Years

Cardell Goodman had little time for reflection. When he was not rehearsing, acting, or taking purses on the highway, he was busy building up his reputation as a great lover. Early in 1677 he was lodging with Mrs. Alice Price, widow, in Great Russell Street, Bloomsbury. We do not know that Mrs. Price had a daughter named Elizabeth—in seventeenth century London, Prices were as plentiful as blackberries—but we do know that an Elizabeth Price, who was at one time Cardell's mistress, appeared on the stage of the Duke's Theatre. If Elizabeth was indeed the daughter of Mrs. Alice Price we could speculate on the possibility that the girl was stage-struck, and that the handsome actor-lodger put her on the stage in return for her favors. But we do not know.

Elizabeth Price, actress, was on the stage for nearly two years and had several other lovers besides Goodman. At length she met Charles Knollys, self-styled Earl of Banbury, who, after many delays, married her in Italy in 1692. After she returned to England, Elizabeth discovered that Knollys had another wife who claimed an earlier marriage. It seems that Knollys and one Margaret Lister were married by Dr. William Cleaver of Croydon, notorious for giving out false or predated certificates. When Knollys asked Elizabeth to sign a disclaimer of her marriage, she refused and brought suit, calling herself the true Countess of Banbury. In January, 1697, after a trial lasting three and a half years, during which Elizabeth's past was thoroughly raked over, the Court of Delegates gave its decision in favor of Mrs. Lister, arguing that Elizabeth Price "had been a player, and mistress to several persons, particularly to coll. Parker, Feilding, and Goodman" and had no children, while "Mrs. Lister was a gentlewoman of good reputation, and had children by his lordship." The Delegates decided that it would be "a great injustice to annul that marriage and bastardize the children." The fact that at the time of the decision Goodman was notorious as a Jacobite concerned with a plot to kill King William would hardly dispose the Delegates to look with favor upon his ex-mistress.[1]

But all this was in the future. Cardell's immediate concern in January, 1677, was with the King's Company, which started the new year with a costly success, Crowne's *The Destruction of Jerusalem*. John Crowne, a poet who had been for some years under contract to the Duke's Company, had so far written four moderately successful plays and the famous masque, *Calisto*, produced at Court by amateurs in February, 1675. We do not know the terms of Crowne's contract, but the chances are that he was paid about forty shillings a week as a retaining fee or pension. Against the sum of this pension would be set Crowne's profits from the third day of his plays. A successful play could wipe out his debt to the company and leave him with a surplus.[2]

For more than a year Crowne had been working on a ponderous two-part heroic play on the theme of the Roman Titus's hopeless love for the Jewish Queen Berenice. Late in 1676, when he brought his finished manuscript to the players, he learned that the Duke's House had already accepted Otway's *Titus and Berenice*, a play on the same theme, which was to be produced in December. Although he was deeply in debt to the Duke's Company, the frustrated author took his play to the King's Players, who accepted it happily. The canny Duke's Comedians said nothing and bided their time. After their rivals had rehearsed the play, and had been put to "a vast expence in Scenes and Cloathes," the managers of the Duke's Company put in a claim for the sum paid to Crowne by way of pension. It was too late to withdraw the play. The King's Company had to pay its rivals £112, and Crowne had to pay out of his own pocket

£40, probably for money loaned him by the Duke's Company. Although *The Destruction of Jerusalem* met with a "wild and unaccountable Success," and was "much commended," especially for its epilogue "that tells 'tis not like to please this age to bring them a story of Jerusalem, who would more delight in one of Sodome, and a vertuous woman which in this age they promise shan't be seene but on the stage," we may be sure that after all costs were paid neither the poet nor the company was much richer.[3]

Crowne's play was a seven-days' wonder, quickly forgotten, and again the company had to fall back on revivals. With the Killigrews, father and son, deep in litigation and with no bright new plays to offer for the spring session of Parliament, when pleasure-seeking gentry came to town, the King's Company faced a bleak season. But on February 22 the courts decided in favor of Charles Killigrew, the son, who became Master of the company and momentarily gave it new life. Then Nathaniel Lee brought the players his overblown heroic tragedy, *The Rival Queens*, the story of Alexander's love for gentle Statira (Mrs. Boutell), and of the efforts of passionate Roxana, (Mrs. Marshall) to get him for herself. *The Rival Queens*, produced on March 17, was a great success and became a stock play. Charles Hart gained new laurels as Alexander, "he Acting that with such Grandeur and Agreeable Majesty, That one of the Court was pleas'd to Honour him with this Commendation; that Hart might Teach any King on Earth how to Comport himself." From his place in the wings, Cardell Goodman watched, envied, and learned.[4]

For the second time since Cardell joined the company, his name appeared in a printed cast of characters; in *The Rival Queens* he played the small part of "Polyperchon, Commander of the Phalanx." One of the conspirators against Alexander the Great, "the haughty Polyperchon" is a dreadful boaster, who cries to his fellows,

> *What can you fear? though the Earth yawn'd so wide*
> *That all the labours of the deep were seen,*
> *And Alexander stood on th'other side,*
> *I'd leap the burning Ditch to give him death,*
> *Or sink my self for ever.*

But he does nothing but stand around and scold, while his friends proceed with the happy business of poisoning Alexander, who dies screaming for the billows of the Tigris to cool his smoking entrails.

A week or so later Goodman played another braggart, Capt. Mullineux in *The Country Innocence*, an old comedy altered for the worse by John Leanerd. This was a "Lenten play," acted by the hirelings only, and, bad as it was, apparently it had some success. Capt. Mullineux' functions were to come storming onstage, kick out three of the foolish suitors for the hand of Lady Lovely (Mrs. Marshall), quarrel and fight with Sir Oliver Bellingham (Lydall), suffer a wound from his sword, and then, in a sudden burst of kindness, help Sir Oliver get the Lady's hand in marriage. The role made few demands upon Cardell. His natural swashbuckling talents were enough to carry him through.

The Country Innocence marked the last known appearance at the Theatre Royal of dark, handsome Rebecca Marshall, the company's leading lady. Three months later she appeared in D'Urfey's *A Fond Husband* at the Duke's House and then left the stage to accept her "kind and welcome Fate"—presumably a lover who set her up in style.

She was only one of many deserters. When the Theatre Royal began to sink, the actresses were the first to abandon ship. The well-equipped Duke's Company had little room for them; even Mrs. Marshall lost face and rank by her move. Luckily, unlike the male hirelings who had no trades to turn to, the women of the King's Company could always fall back on the Oldest Profession. They had only to accept the offer of private lodgings, a coach and pair, and some £300 a year made by one of the lecherous gentlemen who invaded the tiring rooms with fat purses and oily promises. Even the most obscure gentry could become "eminent for keeping one of the players," and were willing to pay sizable sums for the privilege. In 1675 and 76 the King's Company lost Anne and Susanna Uphill, Elizabeth Cox (who returned in 1681), Elizabeth James, Betty Slade, and Mrs. Wyatt—most of them to backstage buyers. In 1677 and 78 it lost Rebecca Marshall, Margaret Rutter, and various lesser light-

THE LEAN YEARS

o'loves. In the epilogue to *The Rival Queens* the players protested to the keepers in the audience that

> *our Women who adorn each Play,*
> *Bred at our cost, become at length your Prey:*
> *While green, and sour, like Trees we bear 'em all,*
> *But when they're mellow straight to you they fall:*
> *You watch 'em bare and squab, and let 'em rest;*
> *But with the first young down, you snatch the Nest.*
> *Pray leave these poaching tricks, if you are wise,*
> *E're we take out our Letters of Reprise.*
> *For we have vow'd to find a sort of Toys*
> *Known to black Fryars, a Tribe of Chooping Boys:*
> *If once they come, they'l quickly spoil your sport;*
> *There's not one Lady will receive your Court:*
> *But for the Youth in Petticoats run wild,*
> *With oh the archest Wagg, the sweetest Child.*
> *The panting Breasts, white Hands and little Feet*
> *No more shall your pall'd thoughts with pleasure meet.*
> *The Woman in Boys Cloaths, all Boy shall be,*
> *And never raise your thoughts above the Knee.*

Even this dreadful threat had no effect; the women continued to leave the theater for the comforts of keepers. In the years 1675–78 the King's Company was forced to recruit, hiring Mary Corbett (sworn in on April 3, 1675), Anne Quin, nee Marshall (November 27, 1676), who soon flitted to the Duke's Company, Ursula Knight (March 12, 1676–7), Katherine Baker (November 10, 1677), Sarah Cooke (*ca.* 1677), and several inept young women—Mrs. Vincent, Mrs. Merchant, Mrs. Bates, and Mrs. Farlowe—who fretted their hour upon the stage and then were heard no more. Of the troupe which had played so admirably before the Theatre Royal fire in January, 1672, only three women were left: Pepys' *bonne amie*, Mrs. Knepp, the singer, little Betty Boutell, the blonde ingenue, and stalwart, durable Katherine Corey, famous as nurse, governess, waiting woman, and bawd.[5]

On May 5, 1677, the King's Company produced Ravenscroft's *Scaramouche a Philosopher*, a farcical blend of Moliere's *Les*

Fourberies de Scapin and *Le Mariage Forcé*. Although the play had been written months before this date, for sundry reasons it had been withheld, and the nap of novelty had been worn off by Otway's *The Cheats of Scapin*, recently acted at the Duke's House as an afterpiece to *Titus and Berenice*. In his prologue Ravenscroft complained,

> *Very unfortunate this play has bin:*
> *A slippery trick was play'd us by Scapin,*
> *Whilst here our Actors made a long delay,*
> *When some were idle, others run away,*
> *The City House comes out with half our play.*

Still, with old Cartwright as the foolish Spitzaferro and Jo Haynes playing Harlequin—"with a huge Sword, and a Girdle stuck round with Pistols and Daggers . . . and Rosy-Cheeks, with great Whiskers"—the farce had a fair success. Cardell Goodman played the important role of Plautino, the manipulator of plots.

Without competition the play might have made a goodly profit for the company. But at almost the same time, after long preparation and the importation of expensive Italian masks, feathers, plumes, and linens, the Duke's Company produced its fourth opera, *Circe*, written by Charles Davenant, with a prologue by John Dryden. It drew the usual crowds of sensation-seeking spectators, who left the King's House half empty. According to Downes, "All the Musick was set by Mr. Banister, and being well Perform'd, it [the opera] answer'd the Expectation of the Company."[6]

The King's Company had no counter attraction. Because Thomas Duffett had turned his facile pen to forgery, it could not even follow its usual pattern of parody. It seems that Duffett, "at the Instigation of the Devill and evill disposed Persons" had "forged and Counterfeited severall Deeds Bonds and other Writings whereby the Creditors of Sr Anthony Bateman and others have beene and are likely to be damnified in their Estates above £20,000." When the plot was exposed, Duffett, "being pricked in Conscience for so wicked a fact," turned King's evidence and received a pardon on condition of discovering "the whole practice." He wrote no more for the stage.[7]

In its eagerness to get new plays, the King's Company sometimes accepted scenarios so badly written that only the skill of the older actors could give them enough spurious lustre to pass current with an audience. But the master players of the King's Company were becoming discontented and sullen. Why should they wear out their lungs for little or no gain? Let the hirelings sweat and suffer; the older actors would play only when they chose. Cardell Goodman's frequent appearance on the stage this year was not entirely due to his merits. Three shareholders played in *The Rival Queens*, none in *The Country Innocence*, and only one in *Scaramouche*. In the next new play, Chamberlayne's *Wits Led by the Nose* (ca. June 16, 1677), no shareholder would play, and Goodman took on the leading role of Antellus, King of Sicilia, a romantic, passionate, and gently asinine hero. Ordinarily such a character would have been created by Hart or Kynaston, but both men were nursing their wounded prides and flatulent pockets.

The fact is that Charles Killigrew was no better manager than his father, and the theatre's finances were growing steadily worse. Early in the summer of 1677, the master players walked off the stage and petitioned the King for the right of self-government. Leaderless, and out of popular favor, the band of hirelings—Lydall, Watson, Haynes, Powell, Goodman, Griffin, Clarke, Coysh, Perin, and Wiltshire—kept on, playing their hearts out to no purpose. Their plight was bitterly described in the prologue to *Wits Led by the Nose:*

> When you come here, as Gad 'tis very rare,
> You serve us like the Monsters of the Faire;
> Hiss without reason, damn without controule,
> As if you meant to Sacrifice the Soul.
> This strange unkindness has our Stage undone,
> And all that you thought Actors faith are gone:
> The men to Misses, Places, or Estates,
> The Women to their kind and welcome Fates;
> Thus both at once retiring from the Stage,
> Have left us here the Objects of your Rage.

This merely added fuel to the flames. Probably Jo Haynes, who spoke the long, rambling prologue and the abusive epilogue to *Wits Led by the Nose* ad-libbed a few choice remarks of his own. On June 18 the Lord Chamberlain ordered his arrest "for reciteing at ye Theatre Royall a scurrilous & obscene Epilogue." Suspended from acting, Haynes fled to Oxford and joined temporarily the Duke of Ormonde's Irish Comedians, who played there during the Act. In the prologue to its next play, Banks' *The Rival Kings*, (*ca.* July, 1677), the King's Company was forced to apologize for Haynes:

> *Forget how you were serv'd last time, and pray*
> *Be kind this once*
> *T'a modest Prologue and a modest Play.*
> *Dreading your anger poor deluded Tray*
> *Has slip'd his Collar, and is run away.*
> *Jo Haynes himself, that shew'd us this dog trick*
> *Has left us all of your displeasure sick.*[8]

Although *The Rival Kings*, a mediocre heroic play on the rivalry of Alexander and Oroodates for the love of Statira, has no actors' names in its cast of characters, there is no question that it was performed by the hirelings alone. "The great Dons of our House," says the prologue,

> *Themselves would fain have had the Play from us,*
> *But frankly and generously our Author stakes*
> *His purse and credit rather for our sakes.*

This is all very pretty, but it seems probable that at the time of production "the great Dons" were all on strike. No doubt Cardell Goodman in *The Rival Kings* played Alexander the Great.

While shareholders and managers quarreled, the theatre remained dark and the hirelings suffered. On July 30, 1677, the King granted the master players' petition for autonomy, with the proviso that "Mr. Killigrewes right to his shares & profitts may be prserved & that he may also have security given him to indempnifie him from those articles & debts which hee alledges he is lyable unto." His Majesty urged that his decision be sent to the company "with all convenience that ye Company may begin to play to support themselves because they suffer every day they lye still."[9]

Nevertheless, the summer passed without profit. On September 28, Charles Killigrew, dissatisfied with the new arrangement, gathered together building investors who, with his own nine shares, controlled all together twenty of the thirty-six building shares in the the Theatre Royal. This group then made an agreement with a number of the hirelings: Watson, Griffin, Goodman, Powell, Carey Perin, Thomas Disney (an ex-stroller and rope-dancer), and Sarah Cooke, in effect setting up a new company which agreed to act only in the Theatre Royal and to pay the rent of £5 14s every acting day.

If this manoeuvre was an attempt to elbow the Old Men (as they came to be called) out of the theatre, it failed. True, most of them were only occasionally active, and by this time Lacy and Kynaston had retired and were living on pensions of 6s 3d paid for every acting day. But among them the Old Men still owned sixteen building shares plus a controlling interest in the scene house, scenes, properties, books, and clothes of the company. With investments to protect, and the desire to shine upon the stage still strong in aging bosoms, the Old Men refused to give way before the pressure of upstart youth.

Behind the scenes some kind of an arrangement was worked out. The facts are obscure, but it seems that Goodman, Clarke, and Griffin were admitted into the ranks of the master players. The other young actors continued as hirelings. At least three of the upstart youngsters had reached the height of their ambitions, only to find the summit clouded with troubles. Now, as actor-sharers, they could worry about the company's debts as well as their own.[10]

The King's Company opened its autumn season with Ravenscroft's *King Edgar and Alfreda*, a tragedy so amateurish that it was hardly necessary for the author to claim it had been written "at least Ten years ago." He must have been a mere child at the time. Two of the Old Men, Mohun and Burt, had major roles in the play. Goodman played "rash, amorous Ethelwold," who dares all for love, cheats his royal master of a beautiful bride, and dies protesting penitence.

Apparently Ravenscroft scraped the bottom of his literary barrel to keep the King's Company going. His hastily modernized version of Ruggle's *Ignoramus*, under the title of *The English Lawyer*, was its next venture. No actors' names appear in the dramatis personae, and the play was obviously a failure. The Duke's Company, which had a large backlog of stock plays, and had produced eleven new plays in 1677—comedies, tragedies, and operas by such popular writers as Behn, Porter, D'Urfey, Pordage, Sedley, and Davenant—had no reason to fear its rival.

But the King's Players, buoyed up by the surge of ambitious youth, were still in business. They ended the year with Dryden's greatest tragedy, *All For Love*, produced early in December. Probably Dryden, who had the play ready before July, 1677, had to make some revisions to fit his characters as well as he could to the changed personnel of the company. No doubt he had intended Mark Antony to be played by Hart, who came out of semi-retirement to act, and Ventidius, the blunt general, to be played by Michael Mohun, who was still working doggedly. But if Alexas, the politic eunuch, was designed for effeminate Kynaston, Cardell Goodman was atrociously miscast in the part. It is still harder to picture blue-eyed Betty Boutell as Cleopatra, the serpent of the Nile, and the comedienne, big Katherine Corey, as a Roman matron. But Kynaston was still sulking in his tent; Rebecca Marshall, a Cleopatra type, had deserted the company, and Elizabeth Cox, an ideal Octavia, had gone to her "kind and welcome fate."[11]

Although contemporary comment is lacking, *All for Love* seems to have been only moderately successful. Properly acted, it should have had a long run, but, with its usual bad luck, the company produced the play just when a troupe of French comedians was drawing crowds at Whitehall. Arriving in London late in November, the Frenchmen began acting about December 5 and continued at Whitehall until April, 1678. With a free attraction close at hand (there is no evidence that admission was charged) the courtiers flocked to the Hall Theatre and, except when a new play was announced, left the pits and boxes of the patent theatres half empty.[12]

According to an old agreement with the King's Players, Dryden was to write for them three plays a year and receive as his pay the dividends from one-and-a-quarter acting shares. (In fact he had averaged less than one play a year.) For some years the flood of dividends had dwindled to a trickle. Now, to keep Dryden happy, the players gave him the profits from the third day of *All for Love*, "as a guift, & a perticular kindnesse of the company." There is no way of knowing how much this gift amounted to. The treasurer's account for December 12 (possibly the fourth or fifth day) shows a gain, after house rent had been paid, of only £22 10s 6d. From this, however, there would have to be deducted the per diem pay of hirelings and servants. Usually on the third day a poet's friends filled the house, and the sum taken in would be sufficient to give the poet a profit of forty or fifty pounds.[13]

But Dryden was not happy. Early in 1678, discouraged by the constant bickering in the King's Company and by his own small gains, he went over to the opposition. On or about March 11, 1678, the Duke's Company produced his next play, *The Kind Keeper, or, Mr. Limberham*. There is no evidence that his former associates protested at this time, and since the comedy, an attack on "the crying sin of keeping," offended some powerful politicians who had it suppressed after the third day, it may be that the King's players were glad to escape the onus of producing it.

While Dryden was peddling *Limberham* to the Duke's Company, Nathaniel Lee brought the King's Company one of his wildest blood-and-lust tragedies, *Mithridates*, produced late in January. Mohun played the title role; Hart was the hero, Ziphares; and Goodman, who always had to take second place when Hart played, was Ziphares' wicked younger brother, Pharnaces, who lusts after beautiful Monimia (Mary Corbett), and, of course, doesn't get her. No doubt Cardell found the character of ranting Pharnaces more agreeable than his role as fawning Alexas, the eunuch.

Early in March the hirelings of the King's Company produced Leanerd's weak farce, *The Rambling Justice*, accurately described in the prologue as "a Dull Lenten Play." Easter (March 31) passed, and the company prepared for full production after its enforced vacation during Passion Week. Just at this strenuous time, the Lord Chamberlain issued a warrant for the King's Messengers "to Apprehend & take into Custody Cardell Goodman, one of His Mats Comoedians for certain abuses & misdemeanours by him committed." On the next day he ordered Cardell committed "to the Porter in the Porter's lodge at Whitehall." The misdemeanors are not listed, and the punishment is not stated—perhaps Cardell too felt the indignity of the lash. His imprisonment was brief; a few days later he was playing Trainsted, "another Gentleman of Newmarket," in Edward Howard's very dull comedy, *The Man of Newmarket*.[14]

Last in the series of new plays this spring was D'Urfey's vulgarization of Fletcher's *Monsieur Thomas*, produced in April as *Trick for Trick, or, The Debauched Hypocrite*. Cardell played the small role of Hylas, "an Inconstant Debauch'd Son of a Whore." Perhaps this was type casting. Old Hart created what may have been his last new role for the company, the character of Monsieur Thomas, a wicked young rake. Not long afterward, "Afflicted with the Stone and Gravel," Hart retired from the stage. Probably the summer of 1678 marked also the retirement of Elizabeth Boutell, who sought shelter (presumably) in the arms of her husband, Barnaby Boutell (or Bowtell) of Parham Hall, Suffolk. She returned to the stage in 1688.[15]

The company was crumbling with decay, and the players were flouting authority. On April 19 the Lord Chamberlain found it necessary to issue a warning against petty pilfering. Clothes belonging to the theatre (he wrote) had been "carried out of ye House & Embezelled by some of ye Company." Sternly he warned the hirelings "that none of them prsume to goe out of ye House in theire acting clothes nor carry any of ye said Clothes out of ye House upon any prtence whatsoever as they will answer the Contrary at theire perills." His order may have put down thievery for the moment, but nothing could put an end to bickering and quarrels. In the prologue to *Trick for Trick*, Jo Haynes (dressed "in a Red Coat like a Common Souldier") complained about the "Civill War" within the troupe, the lack of profit—"We share and share, 'tis true, but nothing's got"—and the frequency of closures,

> *To day we play Great Kings, strutt, bounce and fly,*
> *But e're next Morn the Shop's shut up—God buy.*

To save himself from the general ruin, Haynes proposed joining the troops now pouring into Flanders in preparation for a possible war against France,

> *And if your temper change not instantly,*
> *Comedian Haines a man of Sword shall be.*

THE LEAN YEARS

> *'Tis true, my Loyalty is not preserv'd,*
> *But that in many has for Profit swerv'd,*
> *Besides 'tis better to be hang'd than starv'd.*[16]

Debts were mounting higher. The company owed Robert Baden, who sold copper-lace (imitation gold), £135 12s., Thomas Jolly £54 "for making Cloathes for ye use of ye Company," Aggas and Towers, painters, £40, and Thomas Johnson £45 "upon account." Cardell Goodman's landlady, Mrs. Price, was clamoring against him for a debt of £5 16s "for lodgings and money lent." Creditors were petitioning against Edward Eastland (book keeper) for £9 10s, against Robert Shatterel and Thomas Kent (a scenekeeper) for repayment of "10 guynnyes in gold lent," against Henry Wright (joiner) for £4, and against Martin Powell for £5 17s. Playwrights were taking their best plays to the Duke's Company and giving the King's the leavings, or none at all. Even John Leanard, whose first two plays had appeared at the Theatre Royal, took his third and best, *The Counterfeits* (May 28, 1678) to the Duke's Company.[17]

In the summer of 1678, hearing that Dryden and Lee had taken their joint tragedy, *Oedipus,* to the rival house, the King's Players protested angrily. In a petition to the Lord Chamberlain they cited Dryden's agreement to write three plays a year for them; the income of three to four hundred pounds a year he had gained by them during their best years; the third day's profits they had given him for *All for Love;* and his subsequent promise, made before witnesses, that "they should have the refuseall of all his Playes thenceforward." Now he had broken his promise and "jointly with Mr. Lee (who was in Pension with us to the last day of our Playing, & shall continue) Written a Play called Aedipus, and given it to the Duke's Company . . . to the great prejudice, and almost undoing of the [King's] Company, They being the onely Poets remaining to us." Reminding the Lord Chamberlain how, in a like situation, they had been forced to indemnify the Duke's Company for Crowne's *The Destruction of Jerusalem,* they begged for justice. Subscribed to the petition were the names of the manager, Charles Killigrew, and four sharing actors: Charles Hart, Michael Mohun, Nicholas Burt, and Cardell Goodman. Justice was denied, and *Oedipus,* produced at the Duke's Theatre in October, 1678, "took prodigiously, being Acted 10 Days altogether."[18]

It is very likely that in the summer of 1678, Cardell Goodman, disheartened and discouraged, decided to quit the stage. If so, he returned before the autumn. In one of the Lord Chamberlain's "Establishment" books, which contain lists of the King's servants, Goodman's name is given with the date on which he was first sworn as a groom, June 8, 1676. After his name appears this note: "Cert renned dated Aug: 31: 1678." Usually when an actor resigned or was discharged and later returned to the stage, he had to have his certificate as a royal servant renewed.[18A]

For the remainer of 1678 we have very little information about the King's Company, but a great deal about public affairs which were destined to affect both theatres. On September 6, Titus Oates, Israel Tonge, and Christopher Kirby deposed before Justice Edmondbury Godfrey that a damnable Popish conspiracy was afoot to kill the King and his brother and to restore England to the Catholic Church by insurrection and a French invasion. On September 28, the three scoundrels were examined by the Privy Council, and Oates was ordered to seek out and arrest priests and conspirators. On October 17, the body of Justice Godfrey was found on Primrose Hill with his own sword in his heart. Immediately the cry ran through London that he had been murdered by Papists. The Popish Plot terror had begun.

The Theatre Royal opened in October with Ravenscroft's lurid alteration of *Titus Andronicus*, a tragedy of which the author wrote, "The Success answer'd the labour, tho' it first appeared upon the Stage, at the beginning of the pretended Popish Plot, when neither Wit nor Honesty had encouragement." However, as the Plot hysteria swelled to its full tide in the winter of 1678–79, attendance at both the theatres fell off. Nothing on the stage could equal the excitement of the hue-and-cry after Godfrey's murderers, the trials of Titus Oates' hapless victims, and the bloody executions of alleged traitors at Tyburn. Many of the gentry, fearing riots and Papist uprisings, left town. Of those who remained, some found entertainment at Whitehall, where, in November, the Duke of Mantua's Italian players began to act, continuing intermittently until February,

1679. Even the prosperous Duke's Company was hard hit. It produced only one new play in the late autumn, Bankes' *The Destruction of Troy* (*c.* November, 1678), a dismal failure.[19]

The massive attack against Papists spared no one, not even a poor player who still clung to the old faith. Malignant Titus Oates brought charges against a man who had befriended him, Matthew Medbourne, a Catholic and a hireling of the Duke's Company. Accused of complicity in the Plot, he was committed to Newgate, "and there, lying long without Trial, and in want of all Comfort, ended his days in the worst of Prisons," March 19, 1679. Michael Mohun, also a Catholic, was more fortunate in his friends. On October 30, 1678, the King issued a proclamation commanding all Papists to go at least ten miles from London and Westminster. From Mohun's letter of December 14 to Secretary Williamson we learn that Mohun had begged the King's leave to stay in town, "for if I went [he wrote] ye Play-house must of necessity lye still, I having so greate an Employment in itt." The Council had ordered him a license to remain, but because Mohun was "lame of ye Gout" he had been unable to get the document duly signed and sealed. Presumably at this time Mohun, the last of the Old Men still active, was stage manager for the King's Company.[20]

Cardell Goodman, who cared for neither politics nor religion, rode out the first part of the storm in the arms of a new mistress, with whom he seems to have set up housekeeping. On December 23, 1678, one Daniel Smith sought permission to sue Goodman and "Mrs Sarah Young als [alias] Goodman" for £12 16s "for goods sold and delivered." On January 2, 1679, John Dutton of Whitefriars petitioned against "Cardell Goodman and Mrs Sarah Young als Goodman" for £28 for goods sold but not paid for. "Mrs. Sarah Young" was not a stage name. Sarah may have been an actress, but the tradesmen's use of "alias" means only that, without benefit of clergy, she called herself "Mrs. Goodman," a harmless bit of deception which fooled nobody.[21]

If Cardell's creditors hoped to get their pay from his earnings in the theatre, they were doomed to disappointment. In February and March, 1679, the remnants of the King's Company produced two weak new plays, Bancroft's *The Tragedy of Sertorius* and

Crowne's *The Ambitious Statesman*. The prologue to the second play deplored the loss of the company's greatest actors, Hart and Mohun:

> *The Times Neglect and Maladies have thrown*
> *The two great Pillars of our Play-house down;*
> *The two tall Cedars of the vocal Grove,*
> *That vented Oracles of Wit and Love.*

And in the epilogue to *The Ambitious Statesman*, Jo Haynes complained,

> *But I, and all of us, are fallen so low;*
> *Nothing will keep us but Bum Bailiffs now.*
> *Now no divertisement does pleasure bring,*
> *The Pope has set his foot in ev'ry thing.*

Some time in March, with audiences dwindling, bills unpaid, and "several discords and dissensions arising" among the sharing players, the Theatre Royal closed its doors, "and no Plays were acted . . . therein for some considerable time after." In fact, the doors remained closed for nearly a year.[22]

V

Decline and Fall

Without competition, the Duke's Players should have prospered mightily, but in the stormy years of the Popish Plot few people cared for the theatre. In 1679 the political winds blew higher. On March 4 King Charles sent the Duke of York (a steady patron of the stage) to Flanders with his family and servants. Thereafter he himself gave up his usual amusements while he fought to save his throne. The new Parliament which met on March 6 was dominated by Whigs and fanatics bent on rooting out Popery and excluding the Catholic Duke of York from the succession to the crown. The leader of the Whigs was the Earl of Shaftesbury, their idol the Protestant Duke of Monmouth, the King's oldest bastard, their weapons rumors, pamphlets, ballads, votes, and pope-burning pageants. The good old days were gone when the King, needing votes, had only "to send to the playhouses and bawdy houses, to bid all Parliament-men that were there to go to the Parliament presently." Lacking the patronage of King and Duke, of courtiers and politicians, even the Duke's Theatre suffered. The epilogue to Behn's *The Feign'd Curtizans* (late March, 1679) complained to the audience,

> So hard the times are, and so thin the Town,
> Though but one Playhouse, that too must lie down.
> And when we fail what will the Poets do?
> They live by us, as we are kept by you.[1]

The younger members of the King's Company, no longer "kept" by London playgoers, fled to Scotland. It seems that one

Thomas Sydserf had a small company playing in the enclosed tennis court of Holyrood Abbey in Edinburgh. Hearing that good players were to be had cheap in London, Sydserf sent to James Gray—once a comedian, treasurer of the King's Company in 1678, and since discharged—offering him a job as "Master or Principal of the Company of His Majesty's Comedians or Actors" in Edinburgh, and asking him to bring with him the best of the young players. Gray enlisted Cardell Goodman and Philip Griffin, and sometime in the late spring of 1679 the three set out for Edinburgh. Other actors followed by land and sea. On April 14, 1679, in preparation for their journey, Jo Haynes and Mrs. Elizabeth Roche (a pretty but very minor actress) took out "protection certificates" at the Lord Chamberlain's office, papers as useful as passports on a long journey. Thereafter various other members of the company, including some of the doorkeepers and scenekeepers, straggled off to Scotland, where they found employment and safety from their creditors. Only one young player, John Wiltshire, battered his way into the Duke's Company, perhaps as a replacement for Medbourne, who had died in Newgate. Wiltshire's transfer was legalized by a certificate from the Lord Chamberlain on October 24, 1679.[2]

Left with only a carcass, the Old Men and the Killigrews (Charles and his half-brother Henry) picked at its bones. William Wintershall, whose house adjoined the Theatre Royal "and had a door into the same," secretly let Henry Killigrew into the playhouse to pilfer "Clothes, apparel, and books" at will. Wintershall's death in July, 1679, put an end to this quaint practice. Then Charles Killigrew and William Shatterall tried to dispose of the costumes to help pay off the company's debts—or so they claimed. Someone told the King, who on October 30 ordered Killigrew "not to dispose of the said clothes or other propertyes belonging to the said playhouse," but instead to keep everything safe and deliver an inventory to Michael Mohun. To all appearances, by the autumn of 1679 the King's Company was finished. Of the seven living Old Men, Lacy, Hart, Kynaston, and now Burt had formally retired; Mohun was incapacitated by gout; and Cartwright and Shatterall were suffering from the infirmities of age. King Charles might have taken a hand in the situation, but political affairs were approaching a crisis; he had no time for the problems of theatres.³

How the deserters fared in the mists of Scotland we do not know, but the dour moral climate of Edinburgh was hardly friendly to plays and actors. Moreover, Scotland too was in a ferment, and in June, 1679, the King had to send the Duke of Monmouth with an army to put down a revolt by border Covenanters. The actors' lot improved in November, when the Duke of York, brought back from exile in Flanders and hungry for entertainment, arrived in Edinburgh with his retinue.

Apparently in far-off Scotland the "Company of his Majesty's Comedians" could produce any plays it chose, unconcerned about the rights of the London companies. In his "Prologue to the University of Oxford" (1680), Dryden commented that in Scotland even the former doorkeepers of the Theatre Royal became actors, and with the aid of a feather or two played *The Indian Emperor*—Dryden's own play which, of course, belonged to the King's Company. But the Edinburgh players stole from the Duke's Company, too. In a copy of Caryll's *Sir Salomon, or The Cautious Coxcomb* (1671), a contemporary theatre-goer wrote against the dramatis personae the names of the players he saw in a performance, almost certainly at Edinburgh. According to his scribblings, the fugitive Royal comedians dominated the cast. Sir Salomon was played by Martin Powell, Mr. Single by Mr. Styles, Mr. Wary by Carey Perin, Sir Arthur Addle by John Coysh, and Mr. Peregreen, the juvenile lead, by Cardell Goodman. Mrs. Julia was played by "Sarah" (probably Sarah Cooke), Ralph by "Moris" (possibly George Morrice, a scenekeeper), and Roger and Harry, servants, by "German"—perhaps the Mr. Jermaine who appeared later with the company in London.³ᴬ

At the beginning of the new year the owners of the Theatre Royal, bereft of their rents and assured that "no plays or Interludes could well be shown or Represented" without Goodman, Griffin, and the other young players in Edinburgh, begged Gray to bring them all back to London and offered to pay their traveling expenses. As a bribe to Gray they promised to appoint him again as treasurer of the company. The leaders of the young players reached London early in February, 1680, glad to get back to the fleshpots of Covent Garden. In the following months a few more comedians returned, but some remained in Scotland for another year or two.[4]

The revived but short-handed King's Company opened the doors of the Theatre Royal late in February. The times were far from propitious for a theatrical venture. In the past year the Duke's Company had presented eight new plays which, to judge by the complaints in prologues and epilogues, had been greeted by audiences so small as to hardly pay the costs of production. Now conditions were growing still worse. Whig inspired petitions for a sitting of Parliament were flooding into Whitehall, and monarchy was in its darkest hour. Political libels, lampoons, and pamphlets were pouring from the presses, and the prisons were choked with men accused of complicity in the Popish Plot. Political animosity had risen to such heights that no one, Whig, Tory, or Trimmer, was safe from attack. John Dryden, returning home from Will's Coffee House late one night in December, 1679, was severely beaten by three or four men because of his supposed authorship of a Tory satire. In April, 1680, John Arnold, a magistrate, was attacked and left for dead in the street, presumably because he had been an active priest-hunter. Whig poets, of course, could not get their plays produced, and Tory poets had to contend with Whig cabals and catcalls. Several times during the winter of 1679–80 the Duke's Theatre was invaded by drunken Whigs, "flinging links [torches] at the Actors, calling all the women whores, and all the men rogues," and crying "God bless his highness, the Duke of Monmouth." Once Nell Gwyn (the King's Protestant mistress) was at the Duke's Theatre when a drunken Tory came into the pit and called her "whore." "There were many swords drawn and a great hubbub in the house."[5]

The young men of the King's Company had no illusions about their prospects. In the prologue to their first new play, Crowne's *Thyestes*, a hastily whipped-up tragedy of blood with a very small cast, they said,

> *What cursed Planet o're this Play-house raigns,*
> *Palsies, and Gouts, are all the Old mens gains;*
> *And we young men, e're we have learnt to speak,*
> *Have learnt the Old mens cursed trick, to Break.*

> *Some went to Scotland; they had cunning Plots;*
> *Who went to sell the English wit to Scots.*
> *Scots in that traffic excell you I fear,*
> *Witness their Covenant they sold you so dear:*
> *So these young men are come as wealthy home,*
> *As they return devout who go for Rome.*[6]

No actors' names appear in the cast of *Thyestes*, but the players were no doubt chosen from those who (according to Philip Griffin) signed an agreement with Charles and Henry Killigrew on July 30, 1680. The terms of this agreement were long disputed in chancery, but Griffin insists that the profits of the company were to be divided into six and three-quarters parts or shares. Of these, the Killigrew brothers had two whole shares, Griffin a whole share, Thomas Sheppey half a share, Cardell Goodman a whole share, Marmaduke Watson half a share, Thomas Clarke a whole share, and Martin Powell three-fourths of a share. Whatever the terms, it seems certain that these players, together with Carey Perin, Thomas Disney, and Sarah Cooke, formed a new company (the "Confederates") which had to recruit at once, get new costumes and properties, and find the money to pay rent and wages. The parts in stock plays once held by the Old Men were distributed among the new sharers, and Cardell Goodman had his great chance as the company's leading man. It was chiefly in the next two years that he built up his reputation as Alexander the Great (with Griffin as Clytus) in revivals of Lee's *The Rival Queens*.[7]

The greatest problem was to find new plays. The Duke's Company now had all the best dramatists in its stable—Behn, Dryden, D'Urfey, Lee, Otway, and Shadwell—and John Crowne took them his *The Misery of Civil War*, produced *ca.* March, 1680. However, Elkanah Settle, whose Whiggish bent and hatred for the Duke of York had long made him unwelcome at the Duke's Theatre, now brought the King's Company his first new play in four years, a violently anti-Catholic melodrama, *The Female Prelate, Being the History of the Life and Death of Pope Joan*, produced on May 31. Sexy and sensational, it turned out to be a hit, even though Settle lost the chance for big profits on his third day when "the Duchess of Portsmouth [the King's Catholic mistress] to disoblige Mr. Settle the Poet carryed all the Court with her to the Dukes House to see Macbeth." The dramatis personae lists no actors' names, and conjecture would be fruitless.[8]

Except for *The Female Prelate*, the King's Players scored no successes in the spring of 1680, and their needs were pressing. Backed by the Lord Chamberlain's letters, they applied for permission to play that summer at Oxford during the Act. The Duke of Ormonde, Lord Lietenant of Ireland, had already recommended his own Smock Alley Players, but the King's Company persuaded the King that they needed "such an Extraordinary Encouragement to repair them for some misfortunes lately befallen them." In the face of a royal command, Ormonde gracefully withdrew, but the stubborn vice-chancellor of Oxford tried to discourage the King's Players by limiting their stay to eight days instead of the usual ten to twelve and by refusing them permission to set up their stage in a convenient place. But on June 24 the Lord Chamberlain put their case so firmly that the vice-chancellor, feeling the iron under the velvet, gave in completely.[9]

The company began acting in Robert Wood's tennis court on July 8, opening with a special "Prologue to the University of Oxford," by Dryden. After a jesting reference to the Scots rebellion of June, 1679, Dryden pointed out that the King's Company had been "troubled with Scotch Rebels too." Some were still in Scotland. Of the missing women, "one Nymph"—big Katherine Corey?—"with her single Person fills the Scenes," while another—Mrs. Knepp—"Div'd here old Woman, and rose there a Maid." In Scotland anyone could play, even

> *Our Trusty Door-keepers of former time,*
> *There strutt and swagger in Heroique rhime:*
> *Tack but a Copper-lace to Drugget sute,*
> *And there's a Heroe made without dispute.*
> *And that which was a Capons tayl before,*
> *Becomes a plume for Indian Emperour.*
> *But all his Subjects, to express the care*
> *Of Imitations, go, like Indians, bare;*
> *Lac'd Linen there wou'd be a dangerous thing,*
> *It might perhaps a new Rebellion bring,*
> *The Scot who wore it, wou'd be chosen King.*[10]

Their pockets lined with collegiate half-crowns, paid for performances of *The Female Prelate* and Lee's *Sophonisba*, the

DECLINE AND FALL 71

players returned to London. But their brief prosperity was meaningless. No doubt most of the new sharing actors, bedeviled by unsought advice from the Old Men, who could not stay away from the tiring rooms, worked their hearts out to make the company a success. However, according to Daniel Golding, housekeeper of the Theatre Royal, and Andrew Perryman, the wardrobe keeper, the company was some £400 in debt to various tradesmen, the irresponsible hirelings were still pilfering from the stocks of "Clothes and habits," and even one of the sharers, Philip Griffin, was taking for his own use clothes belonging to the company, "as particularly one French Habit, A laced Coat and Breeches, A Night Gown; besides Hats, shoes, stockings, periwigs, and Trimming, being all of the value of above three score pounds." In addition Griffin and others took various sums of money from the company's till and "spent the same for dinners att Tavernes & otherwise." The company's profits dribbled away through rat holes.[11]

For the beginning of the autumn season, Elkanah Settle ground out another tragedy, *Fatal Love, Or, The Forc'd Inconstancy*. Probably Goodman played passionate, reckless Prince Artaban. The play had no success. Unfairly enough, Settle blamed its failure on the fact that it was "perform'd by the feeble Fragment of a Company," but it is hard to see how the best possible actors could have succeeded with such trash.

Thereafter, chained to a treadmill of stale revivals, the young men trudged on, but until mid-December the only evidence that the theatre was still operating is a doggerel account of "The Battle of the B[aw]d's in the Theatre Royal. December the 3d 1680." Celebrating a hair-pulling match between Mesdames Silence and Stratford, the poet, Nahum Tate, advised the gentry in the audience,

> *Give ore ye Tilters of the Pit, give ore,*
> *Frighten the Boxes and your selves no more;*
> *Two Amazons of Scandalous renown,*
> *Have with dire Combat made this Field their own.*

For once, at least, the audience was entertained.[12]

At the end of the year the company presented Tate's alteration of *Richard the Second*. The actors are unidentified, but

Sarah Cooke, as the Queen, spoke the epilogue. Although Tate changed everything that might be construed as a reflection on the Court, he showed a king murdered and a usurper with only a specious right taking over the throne of England. At this critical juncture in the state, such an action pictured on the stage could put dangerous notions into malcontent minds. At least the Lord Chamberlain thought so and banned the play on December 14, after two performances. The stubborn poet changed the names of all his characters, called the play "The Sicilian Usurper," and succeeded in getting it played twice more in January, 1681, "but the Cheate being found out it was forbid acting again," and the company was punished by a costly ten-day suspension. (Eventually, on March 18, 1682, the play, "corrected & amended," was approved for production.)[13]

In January or February, 1681, the King's Company produced *Tamerlane the Great*, a mediocre tragedy by Charles Saunders, a new young poet. In mid-March, when the King met Parliament in Oxford, the King's Company secured permission to perform again in the university town, now crowded with Members and their partisans. On Saturday, March 19, the King saw a performance of *Tamerlane*, with an epilogue written for the occasion by Dryden, and on the following Monday he saw Wycherley's *The Plain Dealer*. On March 28 the King dissolved Parliament, and the company returned to London.[14]

The chances are that Cardell Goodman was arrested, thrown into Newgate, and charged with highway robbery immediately after his return from Oxford. There are no records of his trial and conviction, only of a pardon granted on April 18, but the wheels of due process could move rapidly in the seventeenth century, and two or three weeks from arrest to conviction would be par for the course of justice.

Later accounts of Cardell's off-stage adventures are confused. Theophilus Lucas's story is that "Goodman had good Wages for his Performances; but not confining himself to his Gettings, he must attempt to Clip and Coin, for which being condemned for his Life, a Petition was delivered to King Charles the Second in his Favour, praying that before he died, he might act the part of Alexander; which being granted, and his Majesty there present, he perform'd it so much to Admiration, that his life was granted him." Colley Cibber tells a very different story: "The Pay of a hired Hero in those Days was so very low, that [Goodman] was forced, it seems, to take the Air (as he call'd it) and borrow what Money the first Man he met had about him. But this being his first Exploit of that kind which the Scantiness of his Theatrical Fortune had reduced him to, King James was prevail'd upon to pardon him."[15]

Lucas was certainly wrong in some particulars. Goodman's wages were never "good," and in 1681 he was charged with highway robbery, not clipping and coining. It is possible, of course, that he earned his pardon by playing Alexander before the King—at the Court of Charles the Second nothing was impossible—but such a dramatic event would surely have been noticed by inquisitive gossips and newswriters. Cibber, paraphrasing Goodman himself, indicates that he robbed only once and was caught. Moreover, Cibber names the wrong monarch. His confusion is understandable. King James also had occasion to pardon Goodman for a brush with the law.

Here are the facts available. At the trial of Sir John Fenwick in 1696 the defense did its best to invalidate Goodman's testimony by raking up his rueful past. Fenwick's lawyers, finding the records of testimony sworn against Goodman in 1681, brought into the House of Lords two of his original accusers to tell their tales again. Thus one Mrs. Anne Cross deposed, "A-going to Salisbury Mr. Goodman robbed me. He owned it to me." Another deponent, Edmond Godfrey, was heard "as to Goodman's stopping him in '80 to rob him, and they fired at each other." The events of sixteen years ago were still fresh in Godfrey's memory. "A minister came to me," he said, "and told me it was Goodman. I saw him [Goodman] in the playhouse after acting. Goodman said, 'I have robbed a thousand times, but never had a bullet shot at me before.'" Surely, if Mr. Godfrey can be trusted, this was not Cardell's "first Exploit of that kind."[16]

The final fact is a warrant dated April 18, 1681, for a "Pardon unto Cardell Goodman of all Felonies, Robberies upon the Highways or elsewhere, Burglaries, Assaults, Batteries and Woundings, whatsoever by him committed before the 16th day of this instant April and of all Indictments, Prosecution, Convictions, Outlawries, Paines, penalties and forfeitures incurred by reason thereof." No fanciful story is needed to explain this document. King Charles was a merciful man, particularly tender toward his own servants. Goodman, identified by his victims, was arrested and sent to prison. His playhouse friends presented his case to the King with the obvious arguments: Cardell was a gentleman, a Cambridge graduate, the son of a clergyman who had suffered for the royalist cause, very necessary to the playhouse, and a proper subject for royal clemency. A King who could pardon Colonel Thomas Blood for stealing the crown jewels from the Tower would not boggle at a mere charge of highway robbery. Indicted and convicted, Cardell pleaded the King's pardon and was set free. He returned after an interval to the playhouse, too late to appear in the next new play.[17]

He may have returned also to his nocturnal prowling on the highways; perhaps he had to in order to live. Certainly there was little to be gained from the Theatre Royal. Profits were so small that early in February, 1681, the company had stopped playing for a while, and, after an interlude, had gone on playing for a week or so at a time. On February 23 the theatre owners and the Old Men had brought suit against the new company, the "Confederates," for unpaid rent. All through the spring the company limped along, gaining from its journey to Oxford, losing in the day-by-day battle with the Duke's Company in London, sometimes dismissing the audience and returning admission fees, putting hirelings and servants on half pay, skipping payments on pensions, and closing down when the profits were too low to cover even a minimum overhead.

Curiously, the Lord Chamberlain's records for 1680–82, which show only three petitions for the right to sue comedians, suggest that the King's Players were prospering. On March 26, 1680, Philip Griffin was petitioned against for £14; on October 26, 1681, Robert Mather, a scenekeeper, owed £5 14s "for meate drink lodging & mony lent;" and on March 9, 1682, Thomas Clarke was in debt to the amount of £6. No doubt the Covent Garden tradesmen had long been refusing credit both to the company and the players.[18]

The production of Bankes' *The Unhappy Favourite* in May, with a cast composed of Clarke, Griffin, Mohun, Disney, Mrs. Cooke, Mrs. Corbet, and Mrs. Quin, who had just returned to the company, helped not at all. In his epilogue to the play Dryden spoke for the despairing players,

> *We Act by fits and starts, like drowning Men,*
> *But just peep up, and then drop down again.*
> *Let those who call us wicked, change their sence,*
> *For never Men liv'd more on Providence.*
> *Not Lott'ry Cavaliers are half so poor,*
> *Nor broken Citts, nor a Vacation Whore.*
> *Not Courts, nor Courtiers living on the Rents*
> *Of the three last ungiving Parliaments.*
> *So wretched, that if Pharaoh cou'd Divine,*
> *He might have spar'd his dream of 7 Lean Kine,*
> *And chang'd his Vision for the Muses Nine.*[19]

Providence had turned its back, and the Muses were starving. The ragged remnant of a once proud troupe could not compete with both the Popish Plot and its prosperous rivals. In an effort to keep the theatre open, the owners agreed to accept half rent (£2 17s) on days when the total receipt was less than £10. The company tried again, but its failure is shown by the amounts taken in on three of its worst days: May 11—£3 14s 6d; May 30 —£3 2s; and June 18—£3 13s. On sixteen other days that spring the receipts were less than the expenses. In a prologue written by Ravenscroft and "Spoken before the Long Vacation," when everyone left town, the actors made a final appeal,

> *What shall we do,*
> *To Live? Faith let us be oblig'd by you.*
> *Come all and pay your Foyes before you go,*
> *Else we must troop to Scotland after Joh—*
> *We by the last advice for Certain hear*
> *That Haynes does head the Rebell-Players there.*

The Theatre Royal closed for the summer, but there was no refuge for the actors in Scotland. True, Haynes was still there, but in mid-July a troupe of Irish actors arrived in Edinburgh and took over Sydserf's theatre. The King's Players starved, or turned to the farce and fustian of the London fairs.[20]

Of course the Old Men suffered with the Confederates, and those who had retired had to do without their pensions of 6s 3d for every acting day. Wintershall had ceased from troubling, and John Lacy died on September 17, 1681, leaving his widow, Margaret, a pension of 3s 4d per day as the return on an investment in the company of £200 made in 1664. (This stipend was to be a bone of contention for years to come.) On October 18, 1681, Charles Hart and Edward Kynaston agreed with the managers of the Duke's Company that in return for 5s each on every acting day at the Duke's Theatre (except for benefit performances) they would (1) make over to the Duke's Company their rights "to any Plays, Books, Cloaths, and Scenes in the King's Playhouse" and to the pensions due them from the King's Company; (2) do all they could to promote a union of the two companies; and (3) refuse to help the King's Company in any way. Kynaston, the younger man, promised that he would do his best "to get free" so that he could act at the Duke's Theatre, at ten shillings per day. One can hardly blame them. No such proposals were made to the other Old Men: Burt, Cartwright, Mohun, and Shatterall.[21]

Somehow the young players lived through the summer and opened the theatre in late October with a revival of Lee's *Mithridates*, "The First Play Acted at the Theatre Royal this Year." But the epilogue written for the performance and spoken by Cardell Goodman expressed little hope. The Theatre Royal was "an old tir'd Jade," said Goodman. What were the players to do—"turn Witness of the Plot? . . . take Orders? . . . Will nothing do?" Perhaps a beautiful woman might help, for, he observed, "there's nothing . . . like that sweet Sex to draw Mankind." Dodging between the scenes, he was back in a jiffy, pulling by the hand long-absent Betty Cox. In a pretty confusion she apologized for her long absence and promised to do her best henceforth:

> *When Grey-Beards Govern'd I forsook the Stage,*
> *You know 'tis piteous work to Act with Age;*
> *Though there's no sex amongst these Beardless Boys,*
> *There's what we Women love, that's Mirth & Noise,*
> *These young Beginners may grow up in time,*
> *And the Devil's in't if I'me past my Prime.*

DECLINE AND FALL

Perhaps there was no sex among the beardless boys of the company, but Cardell Goodman was now a mature twenty-eight. Not long after this date, a poetic scavenger, raking the stews for scandal, came up with this interesting notice of Goodman and Betty Cox:

> *Lett Lumley Coax his Mrs. Fox,*
> *And help his younger Brother;*
> *Let Goodman Pox faire Mrs. Cox,*
> *And all Six flux together.*[22]

Whatever happened to Sarah Young, alias Goodman?

In the autumn of 1681 the Duke's Company was so rich in new plays—Shadwell's *The Lancashire Witches*, Lee's *The Princess of Cleve*, Ravenscroft's vulgar *The London Cuckolds*, and Behn's *The False Count* and *The Roundheads*—that the King's Company had no trouble persuading Tom D'Urfey to write a comedy for them, *Sir Barnaby Whigg; Or, No Wit like a Woman*, produced in November by Clarke, Goodman, Griffin, Powell, Perin, Coysh, and Jermaine, a new actor, and by Mary Corbet, Sarah Cooke, Mrs. Moyle, a new actress, and Sue Percival, the fourteen year old daughter of Thomas Percival, a hireling of the Duke's Company. D'Urfey seems to have written the play with the personnel of the company in mind. By this time the whole Town knew about Goodman's exploits on the highway. He was "a very handsome gay fellow," who flaunted the irresistible mantle of wickedness. In one speech given to Goodman (as Townly) D'Urfey hit off Cardell's public image admirably:

Townly. [To Livia] We are all mortal, Madam, and subject to frailities; but I have this comfort, Gad, I sin bravely and nobly; and like a generous Robber, if I do venture damning, 'tis for a prize of value: Pox, I hate a sneaking Crime, it gets a man no credit.[23]

Hard on the heels of *Sir Barnaby Whigg*, the King's Company produced Tate's alteration of *Coriolanus* as *The Ingratitude of a Commonwealth: Or, The Fall of Caius Martius Coriolanus*, a bloody villain tragedy with strong Tory sentiments. Its success is doubtful, its actors unnamed. But with two new plays in a row, the company's prospects seemed to be improving. Now that the worst of the Popish Plot was over, the audiences were returning, and even King Charles was taking a new interest in drama. In the winter of 1681–82 he saw three plays at the Duke's Theatre. Unfortunately the Lord Chamberlain's records of payments to the King's Company are missing after 1677, but from other sources we know that on November 15, 1681 (the Queen's birthday), the company performed *The Rival Queens* at Whitehall—surely with Goodman as Alexander the Great—that on February 4, 1682, the King went to the theatre to see a new play, Southerne's *The Loyal Brother;* and that on February 22 his Majesty "was pleased to divert himself at a Comedy at the Theatre Royal." In addition, on January 13, 1682, the company entertained the Russian Ambassador and his train at the theatre with the second part of *The Siege of Jerusalem,* and on January 14 the Moroccan Ambassador with Tate's *The Ingratitude of a Commonwealth,* and the Moors again on February 6 with a revival of *Rollo, Duke of Normandy*. Whenever the Moors, in their colorful cassocks, mantles, and turbans, went to the theatre, crowds thronged after, more to see them than to watch the play.[24]

For a first play, *The Loyal Brother*, a thinly disguised political allegory, did rather well. Its success was increased by the fact that Michael Mohun played Ismael (Shaftesbury?), the chief villain, and that the popular Mrs. Corey played Begona, the Queen-Mother. Goodman acted passionate Seliman, the Sophy of Persia (King Charles?), in his usual bravura style, and Clarke was his "Loyal Brother" (York?). The triumph of Tory virtue over Whig villainy was itself enough to bring many a Tory half-crown into the company's coffers.

But a dozen performances do not make a season, and the activity of the King's Company in January and February was only the last rally. The company's creditors were still clamoring, the theatre owners were unhappy, the Old Men were demanding, and the Young Men were quarreling among themselves. The company was now recruited to full strength: the shareholders of July, 1680, plus Mohun, Coysh, Disney, Perin, Jermaine, and Richard Saunders, a new hireling. For women's roles the company had Mesdames Cooke, Corey, Cox, Holton, Moyle, Quin, and Percival. It had competence, if not greatness.

Even Jo Haynes, the last of the rebels, had returned from Scotland in February or March—but not to the King's Company. During his long absence Charles Killigrew had discharged him, and, as Haynes wrote in a rhyming epistle to Madam Nelly Gwyn,

> . . . betwixt mee and you
> I'll have nothing to doe
> With him whom I know
> To mee still a Jew
> To his ffreind never true
> Tho' hee has but a few.

It seems that in Edinburgh Haynes had been living in sin with Mrs. Knepp, whom he described as

> that inchanting Dear Lump,
> That Fountaine of Love so juicy so Plump,
> That delicate Compound of Spiritt & Rump.

She had died in childbed, and Jo, mourning her death and that of his still-born daughter, finally resolved "to go to his own country and live honestly with his own wife." But when he arrived in London he found that there was no place for him in either theatre. After some wasted weeks, Jo wrote a petition in jigging rhyme to Nell Gwyn, begging her to intercede in his favor with the King:

> Now dear Madam Gwin I think it no Sin,
> Get the King but to speak to my Lord Chamberlin
> That in the Duke's house I may once Act agen,
> And I doe assure you if I have leave to Play
> It shall be twice as much in his Majesties way,
> For I will still make it my endeavour hereafter
> To lengthen His daies with Fattening laughter.

Jo's impudence was rewarded. On July 18, 1682, his certificate as his Majesty's servant in ordinary was renewed, and when the new united company set to work in the fall he was a member.[25]

The King's Company (without the help of Haynes) tried two more new plays in the spring of 1682, with little success. Settle's *The Heir of Morocco, with the Death of Gayland*, was a tragedy hastily concocted to capitalize on the popular interest in Moors and the Barbary States. With Goodman as Altomar, the heroic Admiral of Algiers ("the true Heir to th' Empire of Morocco"), and Betty Cox as his agonized love, Princess Altemira, the turgid love-and-honor play may have had some popular appeal, but as literature it is contemptible. Even worse was D'Urfey's version of *Cymbeline* as *The Injured Princess*, perhaps the last new play produced by the dying King's Company. Hopeless of profit, D'Urfey refused to write a new prologue and epilogue; those given with the play are tired, old pieces originally printed ten years earlier.[26]

The end came late in March. Overtures had been made for a union with the Duke's Company, a union to which Hart and Kynaston were already committed. The four other surviving Old Men had little to gain by a merger, but at least they could hope for regular payment of their pensions. To the Young Men a union meant the probable loss of their jobs, and the certain loss of their shares. It is possible that the two groups were arguing the matter on the evening of March 21, when, according to a newswriter, "there happened a difference between the Senior and Young men belonging to the King's play house which grew to such a height that they all drew their swords which occasioned the wounding of severall. But in the end the Seniors shut up the dores and sent word to his Matie in regard they were the builders of the house who received answer yesterday that the Law was open. Where upon they are to have a tryall this Weeke before the Lord Chancellor."[27]

If the cause at issue was the union of the two companies, the aftermath shows that the Lord Chancellor gave his decision to the Old Men. (According to Edward Kynaston, King Charles "did by Express Command dissolve the said Company, and ordered them to unite with the other Company.") On May 4, 1682, Charles Killigrew agreed with Charles Davenant, Master of the Duke's Company, that the two patents would be united and the King's Company would be dissolved within six days. The precise date on which the Theatre Royal closed its doors is debatable. Suits in chancery and difficulties in arranging to turn over the lease of the Theatre Royal to the new united company held up the conclusion of the merger until late in the summer. It may very well be that the King's Company, or at least a selection of diehards, played occasionally during the spring, and it is certain that a group of the players performed at Oxford during the Act that summer. In a prologue "Spoken by Mr. Powel. at Oxford, July the tenth, 1682" the players declared,

> *We the poor remnant of a ruin'd Stage,*
> *Must call the very Storm that wrack't us kind,*
> *Since we this safe, and pleasant harbour find.*[28]

This was the King's Company's last tour. On August 5 a newswriter, announcing a forthcoming visit by the Duchess of York to the Duke's Theatre, added, "that and ye Kings house haveing Joyned Interests the latter being Discontinued." The tragedy was over, but it is possible that the "poor remnants of a ruin'd Stage" tried to continue for awhile as a strolling company. A band of players who called themselves "His Majesty's Servants" acted before the King at Newmarket in October, 1682. Usually when the King went to Newmarket, he "went a-hawking in mornings, to cock matches in the afternoons (if there were noe horse races), and to plays in the evenings, acted in a barn by very ordinary Bartlemew-fair Commedians"—who presented such entrancing plays as *The Fair Maid of the West, or A Girl worth Gold*. If the troupe at Newmarket in October was composed of the last of the King's Players, they had fallen upon evil days indeed.[29]

VI

Barbara

In the autumn of 1682, the new united company, which now called itself the King's Company, had two theatres on its hands, the Duke's House in Dorset Garden—renamed the Queen's Theatre—and the smaller Theatre Royal in Bridges Street. Reserving the Queen's Theatre for operas, the company moved to the Theatre Royal, which had the advantage of proximity to the Court. On November 16, 1682, the united company opened the Theatre Royal with an old play refurbished with a prologue and an epilogue by John Dryden. In his prologue ("To the King and Queen, at the Opening of Their Theatre, 1682") Dryden insinuated that the Duke's Company had been able to take over the Theatre Royal as a "new Plantation" because,

> *The Factious Natives never cou'd agree;*
> *But aiming, as they call'd it, to be Free,*
> *Those Play-house Whiggs set up for Property.*
>
> *Some say they no Obedience paid of late;*
> *But wou'd new Fears and Jealousies create;*
> *Till topsy-turvy they had turn'd the State.*
>
> *Plain Sense, without the Talent of Foretelling,*
> *Might guess 'twould end in down-right knocks and quelling:*
> *But seldome comes there better of Rebelling.*

The managers of the Duke's Company did their best to provide for the "Factious Natives" thrown out of work by the union, but with such excellent actors as Thomas Betterton and William

Smith for heroic parts (Henry Harris retired about this time), Samuel Sandford for villain roles, James Nokes, Anthony Leigh, Cave Underhill, and Thomas Jevon for comedy, and such talented women as Elizabeth Barry, Elizabeth Currer, Elinor Leigh, and Lady Slingsby (Mary Lee), plus a dozen capable and experienced players for supporting roles, there was very little room. Nevertheless, the managers found places for Kynaston, Goodman, Griffin, Haynes, Perin, Powell, Saunders, Mrs. Cook, Mrs. Corey, and Sue Percival. Hart, afflicted by gout and stone, played no more. He died in August, 1683. Mohun, unable to play regularly, petitioned for a pension equal to that given Hart (five shillings every acting day) and won his case. He died in 1684. Cartwright, who played very rarely after the union, lived until December, 1687. Nicholas Burt and William Shatterall retired, and Marmaduke Watson joined the Smock Alley players in Dublin. Of the unwanted members of the old King's Company, John Coysh turned to strolling, and set up a booth in Bartholomew Fair. Clarke, Disney, Jermaine, Sheppey, Mrs. Cox, and Mrs. Holton disappeared from the scenes.[1]

After the union our information about the players is severely limited by the fact that, taking advantage of its monopoly, the new King's Company chose to depend chiefly upon revivals, particularly of stock plays belonging to the disbanded company. The practice made for prosperity, but it penalized the dramatic poets. As Matthew Prior wrote in "A Satyr on the Modern Translators,"

> *Since the united Cunning of the Stage*
> *Has balk'd the hireling Drudges of the Age:*
> *Since Betterton of late so thrifty's grown,*
> *Revives old Plays, or wisely acts his own . . .*
> *Those who with nine Months Toil had spoil'd a Play;*
> *In hopes of eating at a full Third Day,*
> *Justly despairing longer to sustain*
> *A craving Stomach from an empty Brain,*
> *Have left Stage-practice, chang'd their old Vocations,*
> *Attonning for bad Plays, with worse Translations.*

Once upon a time, the players had begged the writer for a new play. Now the shoe was on the other foot; the playwright had to "dance attendance" on the actors, "cap in hand," to get them to produce his play.²

In its first two seasons (until November, 1684) the united company produced only eight new plays or alterations of old plays. Cardell Goodman's name appears in printed casts only for the secondary role of Anibal in Lee's *Constantine* (*c.* November, 1683), for the Emperor Valentinian in Fletcher's *Valentinian* (February, 1684) as altered by the late Earl of Rochester, and for Julius Caesar, with Betterton as Brutus and Smith as Cassius in a Shakespearean revival of 1684. For the first of these plays Goodman had the additional honor of delivering Lee's prologue, a sober essay on the sad lot of the poet in modern society—

> *Tell'em how Spencer starv'd, how Cowley mourn'd,*
> *How Butler's Faith and Service was return'd—*

concluding with an admonition to parents to whip the child who showed signs of wanting to be a poet.

There was some honor, too, in the choice of Goodman to play Valentinian, the lustful Roman Emperor who tries to seduce chaste Lucina (Mrs. Barry), ravishes her, kills his faithful general, Aecius (Betterton), defies Lucina's husband, Maximus (Kynaston), and finally is slain by his own soldiers. *Valentinian* was given a gaudy production right after Blanket Fair, an impromptu city of booths on the hard-frozen Thames, with bull-baiting, ox roasts, fox hunts, races, plays, and interludes. Mrs. Cook spoke different prologues for the first and second days, and Mrs. Barry spoke the epilogue. On Monday, February 11, the play was performed at Whitehall before the King and all the beauties of the Court. Said Downes, "The well performance, and the vast Interest the Author made in Town, Crown'd the Play, with great Gain of Reputation; and Profit to the Actors."³

We may be sure that in addition to these three roles, Cardell performed in a number of stock plays, and he was always in demand as Alexander in the popular *The Rival Queens*. But he was no longer a shareholder, a master player, the leading man of a company. He was a hireling again, at forty shillings a week. His years on the stage had brought him a measure of fame but no wealth. Even the money he had borrowed as a shareholder in the Theatre Royal to buy such items as "Roman habits or shapes for some plays," had gone down with the wreck of the first King's Company, and only the lawyers were likely to realize anything from the properties and books in which he had an interest. Ahead of him were men only a few years his senior but with well-established reputations and fixed places in the hierarchy of the stage. Goodman was really needed only when an old King's Company play was revived, in a part which he had in memory; and even then he played on the sufferance of Betterton and Smith. His position in the new company is emphasized by the fact that about 1684 an anonymous poet devoted most of a "Satyr on the Players" to Betterton, Smith, Nokes, Underhill, and Leigh, and dismissed Cardell with the caustic couplet:

> *Goodman the Thief Swears 'tis all Womens Lots*
> *To dote upon his Ugliness and Pox.*[4]

For nearly two years Cardell, overshadowed by Betterton and Smith, made no progress. At least his forty shillings a week salary was promptly and regularly paid. During these years only the Rye House Plot of March, 1683, a frustrated attempt to ambush the King and his brother on their return from Newmarket to London, disturbed the national peace. The Whigs were defeated, Lord Shaftesbury had fled to Holland and died there, and Titus Oates, completely discredited, was soon to be charged with perjury. Trade was flourishing, and London was prosperous. The King and Queen and the Duke and Duchess of York went to the theatre four or five times a year, and now and then the King summoned the players to Whitehall where there was always good cheer and plenty of beer. The new King's Company was doing very well, but Cardell Goodman had no share in its profits.

Sometime early in 1684 (at a guess) Cardell became intimate with Barbara Palmer, Duchess of Cleveland. At forty-two Barbara was still one of the most beautiful women in England, tall, with chiseled features, clear complexion, blue eyes, dark auburn hair, and a lush body, said to be skilled "in all the tricks of Aretine." At eighteen, after an affair with the Earl of Chesterfield, Barbara Villiers married Roger Palmer, a wealthy law student. At the Restoration, in 1660, she became mistress to King Charles the Second—tradition has it that she "was prepared for his Bed the very first night he lay at Whitehall." In December, 1661, the King created her husband Earl of Castlemaine in the peerage of Ireland.

Separated from her wittol husband and recognized as *maîtress en titre*, Barbara bore the King two daughters, Anne in February, 1661, and Charlotte in September, 1664, and three sons, Charles (later Duke of Southampton) in June, 1662, Henry (later Duke of Grafton) in September, 1663, and George (later Duke of Northumberland) in December, 1665. Some time during these early years Barbara became a convert to her husband's religion, Roman Catholic.

When the King began to lose interest in her, Barbara amused herself with a succession of lovers: among them were Colonel James Hamilton; Henry Jermyn, a courtier; brawny Jacob Hall, acrobat and rope-dancer; and Charles Hart, the actor. In 1670 the King gave her large additions to her pension and the title of Duchess of Cleveland (her husband remained Earl of Castlemaine). A year or so later his Majesty ended his relations with her. His excuse may have been her intrigue with a handsome young soldier, John Churchill, the future great Duke of Marlborough, who is accused of fathering her third daughter, Barbara, born in July, 1672. In the next three or four years the Duchess experimented with more lovers, including William Wycherley, the playwright, and Henry Savile, a gentleman of the King's bedchamber. A satire on her, attributed to the Earl of Rochester, declares,

> *When she has jaded quite*
> *Her almost boundless Appetite,*
> *Cloy'd with the choicest Banquets of Delight,*
> *She'll still drudge on in tasteless Vice,*
> *As if she sinn'd for Exercise;*
> *Disabling stoutest Stallions ev'ry Hour;*
> *And when they can perform no more,*
> *She'll rail at them and kick them out of door.*[5]

In 1676 Barbara went to live in Paris and promptly struck up a match with the English Ambassador, Ralph Montague. Later when Montague tired of her and turned to her young daughter, dissolute Anne, now Countess of Sussex, Barbara shifted her easy

Barbara, Duchess of Cleveland. The National Portrait Gallery, London.

affections to handsome Alexis Henry, Marquis de Chatillon. Malicious Montague peached to King Charles, and when Barbara visited England in the spring of 1678, she was coldly received. On her return to Paris, she wrote to his Majesty an account of Montague's double-dealing and defended her own conduct by pointing out that "as to love, one is not mistriss of one's self, & that you ought not to be offended with me, since all things of yt nature is at an end wth you & I." She reminded him also of his parting words when she first set out for Paris, "Madam, all that I ask of you, for yr own sake, is, live so for the future as to make the least noise you can, & I care not who you love." Had not Montague tattled there would have been no noise.[6]

Whenever the amorous Duchess was not in bed with a lover, she was venturing her guineas at the gaming tables. At Paris in one night she was said to have lost either twenty or forty thousand pounds to a captain of the French King's Guards. It was rumored that she had sold all her property to pay her debts and was about to enter a nunnery. Certainly, although she gave a thousand pounds to the Blue Nuns of Paris, she had no intention of taking the veil. In July, 1679, when the Duchess was due shortly in England for the marriage of her son Henry to Isabella Bennett, daughter of the Earl of Arlington, King Charles warned the Commissioners of the Treasury to look to themselves, "for that [the Duchess] would have a bout with them for money, having lately lost £20,000 in money and jewels in one night at play." She came, saw, and did not conquer, returning to Paris in November as penniless as she came. She was reported to be "scandalous and poor, both to a great degree." Yet she had pensions totaling at least £10,700 a year! While in England she had rented her palace, Cleveland House, to the Portuguese Ambassador. In April, 1682, still in debt but spending as freely as ever, she returned to England, this time to stay, now that the tumult of the Popish Plot was over. Since the Portuguese Ambassador had given up her house, she offered to rent it entire or subdivided into apartments, found no takers, and settled down in it herself.[7]

In 1684 Barbara had been four or five years without an acknowledged lover; she was ripe, ready, and ruttish. Because she was a regular playgoer, she surely must have seen Goodman on the stage, perhaps in his best role as Alexander the Great. School girls who identify the actor with the character he personates and fall in love with a fiction are common enough, and Barbara, for all her years, was impressionable as any schoolgirl. Then too, Goodman, on or off the stage, must have been a fine figure of a man. He was tall, dark, and graceful, and under the soft candlelight of the stage, dressed in a long-coated silk brocade suit, with Flemish lace cuffs and cravat, embroidered gloves, high-tongued shoes with ribbon bows, a fair periwig, a forest of feathers in his hat and a regal truncheon in his hand, he was every inch a hero.

Surely Barbara would identify herself more with proud, passionate Roxana in *The Rival Queens* than with milk-and-water Statira, who was doomed "to die so fair, so innocent, so young." Roxana's unabashed seduction of Statira's husband was not unlike Barbara's success with King Charles, and her frank reveling in the details of sex must have struck a responsive chord in Barbara's breast. For example, recalling her bigamous bridal night with Alexander, Roxana went into an ecstacy:

What said he not, when in the bridal bed
He clasped my yielding body in his arms,
When with his fiery lips devouring mine,
And molding with his hand my throbbing breast,
He swore the globes of heaven and earth were vile
To those rich worlds, and talked, and kissed, and loved,
And made me shame the morning with my blushes.

Barbara was long past blushing, but not beyond luxurious fancies and desires. She too would have an Alexander, a demigod of the green room; she would seduce him to her bed with impious arts and wanton in his arms. She arranged a time and a place, and gentlemanly Cardell, as in his earlier days with "a very fine Woman" in the Strand, "could not be so uncivil as not to gratifie her Desires."

Perhaps both parties to the intrigue had in mind at first nothing more than a frisk or two and farewell. Certainly the Duchess was not noted for fidelity, and Cardell, a true Restoration libertine, had taken his pleasure in a variety of beds. But, strangely enough, the affair went on and on. It is possible that Cardell fell in love with Barbara. She was twelve years his senior, but she was still beautiful, and she had lost none of her erotic skills. Besides she was a DUCHESS with a very large income. Perhaps, too, for the first time in her licentious life, Barbara fell seriously in love. In her lexicon "love" included everything from rape to rapture, and it may be that Cardell met her wishes more completely than any of her previous lovers. Whatever the emotions involved, the Duchess and the player found themselves so well suited that their amour lasted for the astounding period of twelve years, and, but for politics and plots, might have lasted until death.

Early in their association, the Duchess, unwilling to share her lover with the theatre, offered to keep him. He could hardly afford to refuse. His career on the stage had reached a plateau; barring remarkably good luck, he could see himself spending the rest of his life as a hireling at forty shillings a week. The Duchess offered him comfort, security, elegant attire, prestige, and pelf. In another era masculine pride might have made him at least hesitate, but the customs of Restoration society had turned pride upside down. Rich men kept their mistresses openly, and rich women paraded their gallants before the world. The kept actress and the kept actor could alike boast of their dependance—even homely Jo Haynes once asserted proudly in a prologue, "You hardly will believe me—I was kept!" As for precedent—if John Churchill (now Baron Churchill of Aymouth) could accept a douceur of £5,000 from the grateful Duchess, we could hardly expect Cardell Goodman to boggle at a salary paid for services rendered.[8]

To protect herself from scandal, ever the doom of beauty, the Duchess appointed Goodman her Gentleman of the Horse. No doubt because of his long association with horses on the King's highways, Goodman was well qualified for such a post. In a noble household the Gentleman of the Horse commanded a dozen or more footmen, grooms, coachmen, and postillions. He had full charge of the stables and kennels, buying liveries, equipment, horses, and feed, and seeing to the upkeep of the coaches. As his title implies, he was a "gentleman," not a member of the servant class. Goodman went abroad with his mistress, in her coach or on horseback, attended her at Court and on journeys to Windsor, Newmarket, Bath, or Tunbridge Wells, and was acceptable in genteel circles. Ordinarily a Gentleman of the Horse had lodgings in his employer's house, received full board and all his clothing, and was paid in addition some twenty or more pounds a year. However, the chances are that Cardell was paid on a higher scale. Theophilus Lucas tells us only that "Goodman had a good Allowance to live upon from the Dutchess of C[levelan]d."[9]

Whatever the pay, the work was light and reasonably pleasant. Cardell Goodman, son of a poor parson, had reached, if not the summit of earthly felicity, at least a nearby pinnacle. In the eyes of his fellow players he was a man to be envied and admired. To respectable people the sight of the Duchess parading him openly in her carriage was a scandal. In the first version of "The Playhouse. A Satyr" (c. 1684), Robert Gould wrote,

> *Now hear a wonder that will well declare,*
> *How extravagantly lewd some women are,*
> *For even these men* [the actors] *base as they are & vain*
> *Our Punks of highest quality maintain,*   (Cleveland &
> *Supply their dayly wants (which are not slight)*   Goodman)
> *But 'tis that they may be supply'd at night.*
> *These in their coaches they take up and down*
> *Publish their foul disgrace ore all the town,*
> *And seem to take delight it should be known.*[10]

The King's reaction to Barbara's brazen flaunting of her harlotry is not recorded, but he must have been annoyed. She was hardly living so "as to make the least noise possible." Her three sons had even more reason for wrath. For six years, while they were growing to maturity, Barbara had been in France, and they could ignore her gallantries. Now they had to meet her latest lover—a common player, forsooth!—in their mother's house. None of the young men was very bright, but twenty-one year old Henry, Duke of Grafton, was a brash young man with some imagination, no scruples, and a considerable acquaintance in taverns and bawdy houses. He was well qualified to engineer the plot against Goodman which developed in the summer and fall of 1684.

The sequence of events is not clear, but it seems that in June or July Cardell was again arrested and charged with a robbery on the highway, "committed some years since," but presumably after his pardon of April 18, 1681. While Goodman fretted in Newgate, someone (probably Barbara) procured him a pardon for "all robberies," in the usual form. The pardon was issued in

July, in the name of Robert Spencer, Earl of Sunderland, the Principal Secretary of State. Sunderland was a coldly unprincipled man, and one suspects that when the King ordered a pardon issued, Sunderland, for reasons of his own, quietly kept it in his pocket. Certainly it never came into Goodman's hands.

At all events, the law was allowed to take its course. However, Goodman, we are told, was wise in the ways of witnesses and well supplied with cash. It is said that a gift of £100 to the prosecuting witness persuaded him to "take off the prosecution"—that is, to deny his former testimony. The result was that on September 2 a session of the Grand Jury at Hick's Hall returned a verdict of "Ignoramus" to the bill of indictment, and Cardell was set free. Possibly fearing further accusations on the same charge, he went into hiding with friends for a while. In the state records is a memorandum that John Wiltshire and Cardell Goodman were to be found "att Mr. Robert Shotterell's house in great Russel Street in Bloomsbury near Mountague house." There is no apparent reason why Wiltshire's name should have been linked with Goodman's—unless he too had played at highway robbery.[11]

Very soon Cardell was back with his Duchess again, driving blithely about town as if nothing had happened. But Fate had a rod in pickle for him. Someone in high place wanted him done in, and there was never a lack of shady informers eager to curry favor and collect rewards for bearing false witness. An Italian mountebank, one Alexander Amadei, had been knocking about in the London slums for years. Claiming to be a "florentine, an hebrew by the grace of God turned Christian," he made his living in a variety of ways, once even setting up as a teacher qualified to instruct in "the hebrew Chaldick, Rabinith, Talmudi, Strick [Syriac?], Italian, spanish and portugese tongues." Now this savoury character came, or was brought, to Sunderland with an amazing story: that Goodman had tried to hire him to poison two of the King's sons by Barbara, Duchess of Cleveland.[12]

Sunderland took Amadei's deposition to the King at Newmarket in early October. For what followed we can hardly blame King Charles. Still suspicious and embittered after the Rye House Plot, in which his beloved oldest son, the Duke of Monmouth, had had a part, he was in no mood to look closely at an information against a mere player, a twice accused and once pardoned malefactor, who was also the Duchess of Cleveland's paramour.

On October 13 Sunderland sent Lord Chief Justice Jeffreys the following letter:

> The King commands me to send unto your Lopp ye inclosed Information of Alexander Amadei, who being a Foreigner, & not well understanding ye English Tongue hath penn'd it in Latin. His Maty knows very well how ill a Man this Goodman is & is sensible that he woud not be wanting to promote any ill Design. He would therefore have your Lopp examine this whole matter, as well in relation to ye Pardon Goodman was endeavouring to obtain, & ye Escape he made out of Prison, as in reference to ye Particulars contained in ye Information, wherein that you may be ye fuller instructed ye Informant himselfe is directed to attend you. His Maty would have you take such Order herein, as you shall think just and fitting in Cases of such Villany, that ye same may be severely punish'd, according to ye Direction of ye law, and ye Informant protected from any Violence or Injury on this account. His Maty would also have Goodman forthwith seized & kept in Custody, in case your Lopp find sufficient ground for so doing.

With the letter went a warrant to Ralph Young, King's Messenger, to bring Amadei before the Lord Chief Justice. In case the Florentine tried to escape, or even looked as if he wanted to escape, Young was to seize him and carry him to Jeffreys by force. Possibly Amadei was a reluctant witness.[13]

To venal Judge Jeffreys (soon to win everlasting infamy at the "Bloody Assizes" after Monmouth's Rebellion) the intent of Sunderland's letter must have been perfectly clear. The King, believing Goodman guilty, wanted him held in custody and convicted with all the awful formality of the law. Jeffreys was to look into his attempt to get a pardon (perhaps for evidence of bribery), to investigate the "Escape" he made from Newgate when the Grand Jury returned its verdict of Ignoramus, and, of course, to accept Amadei's remarkable charges as the literal truth. By taking the matter directly to the Court of the King's Bench, which had jurisdiction over all other criminal courts (with appeal only to the House of Lords), Goodman's accusers bypassed the Grand Jury and the lesser courts which might not be so amenable to the King's will. Lord Chief Justice Jeffreys, Sunderland's jackal, could be trusted to do his brutal best.

On Sunday, October 20, bailiffs stopped the Duchess of Cleveland's coach in the street, hauled Goodman out, and hustled him off to Newgate. Three days later they brought him before the King's Bench Court (at the far end of Westminster Hall) to hear the charges against him. By chance a planter from St. Kitts, seeking convicts to send to the plantations of the Leeward Islands, was in the Hall that day. He reported that Goodman was "very fine [well dressed], and talked boldly, but the Lord Chief Justice was sharp upon him, and told him he must not huff the Court." As an afterthought the planter added what everyone in London knew, "It is reported that the D[uchess] of Cleveland keeps him."[14]

With Amadei's statement before him, Jeffreys told his fellow justices that "this Goodman was first a player, that there was an accusation against him for a capital offence, that he corrupting the prosecutor he unswore it again, on which the grand jury found the bill Ignoramus, and that since a man swore before his lordship that Goodman had hired him to poison the Duke of Grafton and not only him but the Duke of Northumberland." Goodman pleaded not guilty, and had "five or six there to bail him." As we might expect, Jeffreys found his bondsmen—no doubt fellow players—unacceptable and remanded him to prison.[15]

On November 7 Goodman was brought up for trial. In seventeenth-century England simple criminal trials were usually dispatched in an hour or two. There could be no delays, postponements, or clever legal quibbles. By special favor the accused could consult a lawyer, but he had to conduct his own defense in court. The prisoner stood alone in a dock, facing across the court twelve good men and true in the jury box [i.e., freeholders whose property was worth at least £10 a year], while the justices in their scarlet gowns and white wigs looked down upon everybody from their high seats and interpreted the law as they pleased. The attorney-general (Sir Robert Sawyer in 1684) conducted the case for the crown, and usually the prisoner knew nothing in advance about the evidence against him. The fact that an accuser took his oath on the Bible before testifying was accepted as proof that he was telling the truth; thereafter it was up to the prisoner to prove his own innocence.

When the trial began, a clerk read the charge to the jury: that "Cardell Goodman . . . being a Person of a Wicked Mind, and of an Ungodly and devilish Disposition, and Conversation . . . did solicite, perswade, and endeavour to procure one Alexander Amydei, to prepare & procure two Flasks of Florence Wine, to be mix'd with deadly Poison, for the poisoning of the Right Noble Henry, Duke of Grafton, and George, Duke of Northumberland." Then Amadei was sworn and testified that "being intimate with Goodman he went to vissitt him in Newgate when Comitted for a Robbery & Goodman desired his assistance in paying the prosecutrs sister £100 to take off the prosecution." Amadei refused to engage in such a wicked business, and claimed that he "knew not whether it was paid." The jurors, of course, could believe what they chose—or rather what Judge Jeffreys told them to believe.

"After Goodman was discharged," said Amadei, "he desired [me] to prepare 2 fflasks of the Best fflorence wine with poyson to be administered to the Dukes of Grafton and Northumberland." Amadei's initial reward was to be £40 for the poisoned wine. If the results were as desired, Goodman was to give him an additional £100 and to maintain him overseas for the rest of his life.

Goodman denied everything, of course, but it was his word against the Italian's oath. As the jury saw accuser and accused there was little to choose between them. One was a foreigner and therefore not to be trusted; the other was a player and therefore a liar by profession. No supporting evidence was brought in; no other witnesses were examined; and even the intended victims were not called to say what, if anything, they knew. A set of sensible jurymen would have laughed at Amadei's yarn. It was all too pat and romantic—two "fflasks," forsooth, one for each duke, and "fflorence wine," uncommon in England but a label suggestive of decadence, lust, Medici, and murder. Moreover, no one seems to have inquired what possible motive Goodman might have had for wishing to poison the two young dukes—surely not to endear himself with their mother, his mistress! If he had quarreled with them, or wanted revenge for an insult or an injury, he might have had a motive for employing a poisoner. A common player, even though a gentleman by birth, could not challenge a royal duke to a duel. But in fierce Judge Jeffrey's court jurymen asked no questions; they merely did what he told them to do. "In fine, the Jury brought [Goodman] in guilty" of a high misdemeanor. On November 24 Judge Jeffrey sentenced the actor to pay a fine of £1,000 and to find securities for his good behavior for life.[16]

Since Goodman could not pay the fine—he might as well have reached for the moon!—Judge Jeffrey sent him to the King's Bench prison, the Marshalsea. There he could lie until he rotted to his grave. The Duchess, by straining all her resources to the utmost, might possibly have paid the fine, but her extravagance and losses at the gaming tables had completely drained her purse, and she was deeply in debt. This should have been the end of Mr. Goodman, the player.

Nonetheless, although the fine was never paid, Cardell was free two months after his conviction. On January 16, 1685, the Earl of Sunderland wrote to the Attorney General "By his Maties Command." After reciting the facts about Cardell's conviction and fine, Sunderland concluded (writing, of course, at the King's dictation), "We have thought fit to signifie our Will and Pleasure to you, that you forthwth cause satisfaction to be acknowledged upon Record of the said Judgement for the said sume of one thousand pounds as likewise to excuse and discharge his giving Security for the Peace and good behaviour, which we are graciously pleased to remit to him the said Cardell Goodman." This was such an unusual order that the Attorney General hesitated to obey without the consent of the Lords of the Treasury, who might reasonably object to being cheated of a thousand pounds. But on February 4 Henry Guy, Secretary to the Treasury, wrote him that consent had been given, and he was to record the fine as paid. When all the formalities had been satisfied, Cardell was set free, sometime late in February.[17]

No one can be sure what happened behind the scenes at Whitehall, or why the King chose to remit Cardell's fine instead of granting him an outright pardon. At the trial of Peter Cooke in May, 1696, the defense lawyers, to discredit Goodman's testimony, cited his conviction on a charge of attempted poisoning.

The King's counsel replied that Goodman had been "wronged by a causeless prosecution, and the verdict against him was found not credible." Found by whom? Was the King trying to save face for Lord Jeffreys? Was he protecting one of his natural sons? Or, more probably, did he yield grudgingly to Barbara's pleadings, agree to restore her lover, but refuse to give him a pardon? There is no deponent to tell us now. All we know is that after a total of four months in the noisome cells of Newgate and the Marshalsea, Goodman came forth into the sunshine with his reputation permanently damaged.[18]

VII

Libels and Lampoons

In February, 1685, when Cardell Goodman came blinking out of prison, he had reason to thank his stars that he was no longer dependent on the playhouse for a living. On February 7 King Charles the Second died, and two weeks later the Lord Chamberlain closed the theatres for an appropriate period of mourning. Since he did not allow them to open until April 27, four days after the coronation of King James the Second, the poor players had an additional reason to mourn. Later in the spring, when the King's Company had gone into full production, it suffered another blow. On June 6 the players produced at great expense Dryden's new opera, *Albion and Albanius*. In the middle of its run came the news of Monmouth's landing at Lyme (June 11), and, as Downes the prompter complained, "The Nation being in a great Consternation, [the opera] was perform'd but Six times, which not Answering half the Charge they were at, Involv'd the Company very much in debt."[1]

Monmouth's rebellion was quickly crushed, but it was a long time until the company's debts were paid. In fact, the actors never prospered after 1685 as they had in the first golden days of good King Charles the Second. King James, like his brother, patronized the theatres, and at the beginning of his reign he commanded plays at Whitehall "every Weeke." Ordinarily, too, he was not ungenerous to the players, even though, rather meanly for him, he paid off his brother's small debt to the company "at the rate of five pounds [instead of the usual ten to twenty] for each play acted at the Theatre before His late Mats death," thereby saving a neat £55. But quite unintentionally James damaged the theatres almost beyond repair. Under the pressure of his bigoted crusade to restore England to the Catholic Church, the Restoration coterie of aristocrats and wits, who had long been the chief support of the stage, broke up and drifted away, leaving drama at the mercy of mediocrity and the theatres half empty.[2]

The Duchess of Cleveland also found life harder after the death of her regal lover and former keeper. Nevertheless, although deeply in debt and with her future insecure, she still found money for Goodman. Apparently she refused to believe the charges against him and not only took him to her bed again but begged King James to pardon him for all his past misdeeds. James's pardon, issued to Cardell on October 22, 1685, absolved him "of all Robberies and Felonies, Wilful murther excepted, and of all trespasses and misdemeanours by him committed before the 20th day of this instant October, and of all indictments, Convictions, outlawries, Paines, & Penalties incurred by reason thereof." By this all Cardell's civil rights were restored, and the Duchess could show her purified paramour about town in her coach again.[3]

Cardell's resignation from the King's Company closed one of our best sources of information about him. For the next ten years he and his Duchess did nothing sufficiently noteworthy to attract the attention of newswriters. However there were still gossips to give us an occasional glimpse of their doings, and a host of Court satirists who found them worthy of comment and invective.

The writers of libels and lampoons—personal satires in doggerel ballad verse—were the ancestors of modern tabloid journalists and gossip columnists. Usually their poetic products were handed about the Court and Town in manuscript, or were copied and sent to country correspondents. Those with political overtones often found their way into print. Although the Court libelers professed moral purposes, they were, in effect, social satirists, attacking those who deviated from the social norm. They had keen noses for scandal, and were adept at sniffing out lechery. They gloried in, and sometimes invented, the sordid details of an intrigue, but they rarely accused without reason.

The libelers leave no room for doubt that the intrigue between

Goodman and the Duchess of Cleveland continued to flourish. For example, Robert Julian, styled "the Secretary to the Muses," announcing his retirement in "Farewell to the Muses. 1685," declared that he no longer cared to castigate vice and was content to "Let Cleveland to sham Alexander stick." A few months later, in "The two Tom Lucys," an anonymous libeler hinted that Goodman was behaving like a stepfather to the Duchess's youngest son, the Duke of Northumberland:

> *Young widows & mayds*
> *Now hold up your heads,*
> *There are men to be had for all uses.*
> *But who cou'd presage*
> *That ever one age*
> *Shou'd be furnisht wth two Tom Lucys.*
>
> *Noe reason I see*
> *Our Goodman shou'd be,*
> *Soe very much angry with her sonn,*
> *For though her estate,*
> *Be encomber'd with debt*
> *She allwayes was free of her person.*[4]

Although the pronouns are confusing, we may take it that the first "her" refers to the Duchess of Cleveland and the second to Northumberland's new bride. In the spring of 1686 Northumberland was "bubbled into marriage" with a woman of doubtful fame, Catherine Lucy, widow of Captain Thomas Lucy of Warwickshire. The whole Court was appalled by the misalliance. Mrs. Lucy's estate was "encomber'd with debt," and she was "rich only in buty, which tho much prised, will very hardly maintain the quality of a Duchess." When King James expressed his displeasure, the reckless Duke of Grafton advised his brother to get rid of his bride and helped him kidnap her to France, where the two dukes placed her in a nunnery. Eventually, of course, public opinion and the law forced the young men to bring her back to England, where she took her rightful place at Court.[5]

While this scandalous escapade was still in progress, a Court gossip brought the Duchess of Cleveland into the lurid picture. On April 3, 1686, Peregrine Bertie wrote, "We have received an account of the two Dukes being safely arrived at Ostend. As soon as they returne they will be taken into custody by my Lord Chief Justice's warrant, and must give in baile for [the new duchess's] appearance or goe to prison. In the mean time their gratious mother is brought to bed of a son which the towne has christned Goodman Cleveland."[6]

We may take the last statement as evidence that the liaison between Barbara and Cardell continued, but we need not accept the alleged birth as a fact. We hear nothing more about "Goodman Cleveland." Unless we are willing to believe the malice of a later scandal monger, who insisted that the fruitful Duchess of Cleveland had had many bastards—"Incognito within Incognito"— most of whom were carried away under her coachman's cloak, we can only conclude that the rumor was false. It is confirmed by no newswriter and by none of the Court libelers, who would have seized upon the birth with glad cries and turned it into a miracle. A miracle it would have been, indeed. Barbara was nearly forty-five. Her last child had been born fourteen years ago, yet since that event she had had a succession of lovers. Either she was too old for childbearing or, like most of the promiscuous ladies of the time, she had become sterile as the result of venereal disease— "the pox."[7]

But "Goodman Cleveland's" putative father certainly continued in the Duchess's good graces. In the summer of 1686 he was seen walking hand in hand with her at the fashionable spa, Tunbridge Wells. A Court libeler, scandalized at the sight of a duchess strolling with a comedian, suggested that his readers come with him to "the Intriguing Grove,"

> *There wth contempt and scorn behold*
> *The Proud Aurelia now grown old*
> *The quondam great Sultana of the land.*
> *So mean her spirits now are grown*
> *Stoop to a dunghill from a Throne*
> *Now walk with Rakehell Goodman hand in hand.*
> *Besides so Ugly he would be*
> *Ador'd in China for a Diety.*
> *Unbridled lust in this Example View*
> *What will it not provoke some Women to.*[8]

LIBELS AND LAMPOONS 101

The Court libelers continued to attack the Duchess on the slightest pretext; she was always fair game. For example, there was "On the Dutchess of Portsmouth's place Expos'd for sale" (*c.* 1686), a reprise of "Colon, 1679," brought up to date. Among other would-be purchasers,

Cleveland offer'd down a Million
But was told of her pock-fret Stallion   (*Mr Goodman the*
At the very name she fell a weeping   *Player which she*
And swore she was undone by keeping   *keeps as a Stallion.*)
That Jermin & Churchill had so drain'd her,
She could not live on the remainder.

And from "Madam Le Croy" (*ca.* 1687); an attack on several Court ladies, we learn that,

With wither'd Hand and Wrinkled Brow
Cleveland in rage comes next, to know
What desperate Taterdemallion
Should next vouchsafe to be her Stallion.
But by the Wrinkles on her Brow,
She's told her Charms quite fail her now;
And since she coupled with a Strowler,
Her next Admirer must be Jowler.

Finally, if we need further confirmation that Cardell continued as the Duchess's companion, we have the fact that on January 15, 1687, when Barbara granted the reversion of two-thirds of the manor of Woking to her son, the Duke of Grafton, one of the witnesses to her signature was Cardell Goodman.[9]

Significantly, every Court libeler stressed the fact that Barbara had stooped "to a Dunghill from a Throne," or, as one scandal-monger wrote, "It was a mighty downfall from being the darling of a M[onar]ch to become the Mistress of a Com[edia]n." In her own right the Duchess of Cleveland was a proper subject for satire. She had been a target in the days when King Charles had poured gold into her easy lap, when she had acted in a play at Whitehall "adorned with jewels to the value of £200,000, the Crowne Jewells being taken from the Tower for her," and when politicians had blamed all the ills of the nation upon her and the other "cattle" at Whitehall. Once she had been "the Prerogative

Whore," to be flattered, caressed, hated, and libelled. She was roundly cursed for her lust, her extravagance, and her pride. "O Barbara!" wrote the Earl of Dorset,

> *thy execrable name*
> *Is sure embalm'd with everlasting shame.*

Now the libelers had a new stick to beat her with. If the Duchess had been content to lie only with lords, they might have passed over her affairs with no more than a sneer. All but the most godly (who seldom came to Court) looked with indulgence upon mere carnality. But Barbara had betrayed her class; she had chosen to sleep with a comedian, a common player, "a stroller," "a vagabond."

To sharpen the sting of their strokes, the libelers had to denigrate Goodman to the gutter. According to modern standards his morals were far from admirable, but it is hard to believe that he was as black as the satirists painted him in their eagerness to defame the Duchess. For them it was enough that he was a common player; the adjectives "pock-fret" and "rakehell" were automatic additions. He was the stick with which the Duchess was beaten, and his reputation suffered with every blow.[10]

Although Cardell was living in luxury, he never quite gave up the theatre. Lucas tells us that "sometimes for his diversion he would play a Part," and that at benefits for the hirelings he would play "Alexander for them Gratis." Thomas Davies heard that "Goodman, long before his death, was so happy in his finances, that he acted only occasionally, perhaps when his noble mistress wished to see him in a principal character; for Goodman used to say 'he would not act Alexander the Great but when he was certain that the Duchess would be in the boxes to see him perform.' " Cibber remarks that Goodman, unwilling to break his links with the theatre, "often came to a Rehearsal for amusement." Cibber is referring to the period from 1690 to 1695, while the King's Company still had a monopoly, and Cibber himself was only a young hireling. Once, said Colley, Goodman, "having sate out the *Orphan* the Day before, in a Conversation with some of the principal Actors enquir'd what new young Fellow that was whom he had seen in the Chaplain? Upon which Monford reply'd, That's he, behind you. Goodman then turning about, look'd earnestly at me, and, after some Pause, clapping me on the Shoulder, rejoin'd, If he does not make a good Actor, I'll be d——d." Naively Colley added, "The Surprize of being commended by one who had been himself so eminent on the Stage, and in so positive a manner, was more than I could support; in a word, it almost took my Breath, and (laugh if you please) fairly drew Tears from my Eyes!"[11]

For the most part Goodman's rare appearances on the stage went unrecorded, but on February 6, 1686, Peregrine Bertie wrote to the Countess of Rutland, "Thursday was acted Mith[r]idates for the Queen and Goodman played." The fact that Bertie thought it unnecessary to explain who Goodman was or why his playing deserved mention is adequate evidence that he played with some frequency. Moreover, contemporary allusions to him as "Mr. Goodman, the player," "sham Alexander," and "Alexander the Great" continued. Actors are quickly forgotten, and popular titles—complimentary or ironic—have a way of wearing out unless they are frequently renewed.[12]

In the late 1680's, then, Cardell, while enduring the insults of jaundiced libelers, was living well, enjoying life, and indulging his taste for fine clothes. (On April 5, 1689, Robert Hooke noted in his diary, "Mett C. Goodman in M[oor] F[ields], very gallant.") He had given up his nightly forays on the highway and, according to Lucas, had become, like his mistress, "a great gamester at cards, especially L'ombre." With time hanging heavy on his hands, he was often in the tiring rooms of the Theatre Royal, and occasionally played a part for his own or Barbara's amusement. In short, he was living the careless life of a Town gallant, with one foot in the theatre.[13]

He even managed to get involved in a duel. On February 16, 1687, John Dryden sent a letter of compliment and news to Sir George Etherege, Envoy at Ratisbon. "The Coffeehouse [in Covent Garden] stands certainly where it did," he wrote, "& angry men meet in the Square sometimes, as Abercomy and Goodman lately did, where they say Alexander the great was wounded in the arm, by which you may note, he had better have been idle." According to another source, the field of battle was behind the scenes at the theatre. The victor was Duncan Abercromy, a captain in the Duke of Grafton's first regiment of footguards. Abercromy, sometimes referred to simply as "Duncan" or "Duncomb," a profane, roistering fellow, was one of the duke's cronies, and on February 2, 1686, had been his second in a duel in which Grafton slew John Talbot, brother of the Earl of Shrewsbury. The occasion for a duel between Abercromy and Goodman is nowhere stated; it is barely possible that Grafton engaged Abercromy to get rid of Goodman.[14]

Apart from his mishap in a duel, Cardell was a very fortunate man during these years. Famous as a player, he was now equally famous as a lover. In the spring of 1688 an expanded lampoon called "The Session of Ladyes" floated about the Town in manuscript and was copied into the commonplace books which gentlemen kept as repositories for jokes, epigrams, songs, and satires. Following the pattern of a host of "sessions" poems, this libel set up a session of ladies on the stage of the theatre with various ladies pleading before Cupid their claims to "Adonis the Beauty for whom they engage." In the final stanzas Adonis turns out to be thirty-five-year-old Cardell Goodman. Apparently Cardell could be handsome or ugly according to the bias of the satirist.[15]

The author of "The Session" asserts that:

> *Tho' such an Adonis before was not known,*
> *He exceeded the other in Beauty & Grace;*
> *With Age and diseases tho' impotent grown,*
> *He Resembled the other exactly in Face.*
>
> *To this New Adonis, in Park, & at Plays,*
> *Whose Eyes had the Power of Life, and of Death,*
> *Each beautiful Lady an Altar did Raise;*
> *But all their perfumes cou'd not sweeten his Breath.*

To win Adonis's favor, the ladies flocked from Court, stage, and stews. There were notorious women from all three places: Mall Hinton, Mall Howard, Betty Boutell (who returned to the stage this spring), Betty Cox, Elizabeth Barry, and even a famous bawd, Mrs. Cuffly, who "broke her neck in a chair, Making over much haste to put in her claim." All praised Adonis's virtues, and (perhaps with reference to Goodman's stage roles),

> *One took him for Pompey, another for Caesar;*
> *That he Alexander was another strait swore;*
> *And thought he cou'd do as great Wonders to please her,*
> *As the great Triumvirate mencon'd before.*

The true purpose of the satirist was to libel as many Court ladies as possible by picturing them as lecherous, greedy, and vicious. Therefore, among those who put in their pleas, were the Duchess of Norfolk, already notorious for her affair with a Dutch adventurer, Sir John Germaine; the widowed Duchess of Richmond, once admired by King Charles and now pursued by Court rakehells; her demi-rep sister, Mrs. Sophia Bulkeley, wife of Henry Bulkeley, Master of the King's Household; and even the young Duchess of Grafton, who pleaded her need for a male "Since Lusty Tarpaulin [the duke] was sent out to sea" as commander of a fleet in the Mediterranean.

> *This Plea wou'd have took, but the Court was inform'd*
> *That his Grace was with Duncan arriv'd in the Downs;*
> *At the Name of that Hero, Adonis he storm'd,*
> *Being scarcely recover'd of his Dressing Room Wounds.*

More ladies pressed their claims: the Italian Duchess of Mazarine, the ill-used Duchess of Northumberland, the Countess of Mulgrave, old Lady Bellasis, the Countess of Dorchester (King James's cast mistress), Lady Mary Tudor and her mother, Moll Davis (ex-actress and once mistress of King Charles), and a dozen more. Cupid found fault with each. One was guilty of drunkenness, another of excessive lechery; one was too old, another too ugly; one gambled, and another was poor. Finally "Dame Venus herself arrived at the Court" and scolded her son Cupid for exposing such a Beauty for sale to mere mortals. Abashed, Cupid

> *layd by both his Bow and his Dart,*
> *Which at his own Mother he drew to the Head;*
> *And with One Word, she (Resigning her Heart)*
> *To Cleveland put Rakehelly Goodman to bed.*

> *This startled the Court, to see her so pleas'd,*
> *From a Dish for a Monarch, & feeding so Nice,*
> *But all in a Moment the Court was appeas'd,*
> *Since the Goddess had made so equal a choice.*

All through the reign of James the Second, the satirists maintained their chorus. Yet Cardell and his Duchess lived quietly, almost as man and wife. Cardell was still unmarried, and Barbara had been separated so long from her husband that she must have found it hard to remember she had one.

In the summer of 1688 the Court libelers had new matter for satire. On June 10 a son was born to the Queen. The Whigs, refusing to accept the reality of the birth, insisted that an infant had been brought to the Queen's bedroom in a warming pan. A host of ballads on "the warming pan baby" filled the troubled air. More important was the fact that the Whigs, facing a continued line of Catholic kings, invited William, Prince of Orange (the King's son-in-law) to come to England and defend the Protestant religion. The end of the year saw crisis after crisis: King James's hasty attmpts to repair the damage done by his bigotry, William's landing with a Dutch army at Torbay on November 5, and King James's flight to France on December 23.

With the new year, a Convention Parliament, the coronation of William and Mary (April 11, 1689), and temporary political peace, the Court satirists remembered the Duchess of Cleveland again. In "Satyr on Bent[inck] &c.," 1689, for example, she was compared with another lady of pleasure, popular Nell Gwyn, who had died in November, 1687, leaving her property to her son by the King, Charles, Duke of St. Albans:

> *Nelly is dead, and left St. Albans more*
> *Than Cleaveland can her Bastards or the Poor,*
> *A Duchess tho' she dy, and Goodman's Whore.*
> *Who can to such a spend thrift grant Relief,*
> *That gives her Children's Birth Right to a Theif.*
> *The vaunting vagabond lives high, looks Great,*
> *While she not plays, but begs Gold at Basset,*
> *Pretending 'tis a Purse for Charity,*
> *Indeed it is, since her it must supply.*
> *In Goodman's grave may Fate her Carcass lay,*
> *And every Man avoid that foul high-way.*[16]

A year or so later, Robert Gould revised his "The Playhouse, a Satyr," and pointed up his attack upon Goodman and the Duchess:

> *Now hear a Wonder and 'twill well declare*
> *How resolutely lewd some Women are;*
> *For while these Men [the actors] we thus severely use,*
> *Our Ladies differ hugely from the Muse;*
> *Supply their wants, and raise 'em from Distress,*
> *Advanc'd ev'n for their very Wickedness.*
> *Goodman himself, an Infidel profess'd,*
> *With Plays reads Cl[evelan]d nightly to her Rest:*
> *Nay in her Coach she whirls Him up and down,*
> *And Publishes her Passion to the Town,*
> *As if 'twere her Delight to make it known.*

The picture of Goodman reading his Duchess to sleep is too domestic to contemplate.[17]

Apparently the gossips and libelers missed a scandalous event early in 1691. The Duchess had given up Cleveland House and moved to a smaller dwelling in Arlington Street. There, on May 31, 1691, Lady Barbara Fitzroy, the Duchess's eighteen year old daughter, was delivered of an illegitimate son. The father was James Douglas, Earl of Arran (the future great Duke of Hamilton). The Duchess brought the boy up as her grandson, calling him James Hamilton, and sent her daughter to spend the rest of her life in a French nunnery. The birth must have been kept secret; knowledge of it would have stirred up a hornet's nest of lampoons.[18]

No one seems to have had a good word for the Duchess, not even those whom she helped and favored. About 1693 she met and befriended a young adventuress, Mary de la Riviere Manley, who at the age of fourteen had been seduced into a false marriage and had lived ever since by her wits. Years later, in an autobiographical *roman à clef*, *The Adventures of Rivella* (1714), Mrs. Manley returned evil for good. She described the Duchess (under the name of Hilaria) as "querilous, fierce, loquacious, excessively fond or infamously rude. When she was disgusted with any person, she never fail'd to reproach them with all the bitterness and wit she was mistress of, with such malice and ill-nature that she was hated not only by all the world, but by her own children and family; not one of her servants but would have laugh'd to see her lie dead among them, how affecting soever such objects are in any other case. The extremes of prodigality and covetousness; of love and hatred; of dotage and adversion, were joyn'd together in Hilaria's soul." How Mrs. Manley managed to live more than six months on the bounty of this harpy passes comprehension.

Of course she met Cardell Goodman frequently, although, she said, "that beloved person had always a hatred and distrust of Rivella [Mrs. Manley]. He kept a mistress in the next street, in as much grandeur as his lady. [According to the key, this was Mrs. Wilson, of the Pope's Head tavern in Cornhill]. He fear'd she would come to the knowledge of it by this new and young favourite, whose birth and temper put her above the hopes of bringing her into his interest, as he took care that all others should be that approached Hilaria. He resolved, how dishonourable soever the procedure were, to ruin Rivella, for fear she should ruin him; and therefore told his Lady she had made Advances to him, which for her ladyship's sake he had rejected." For this and other reasons the two ladies quarreled, and Rivella left Hilaria's house, never to return. So, at least, says Mrs. Manley, novelist, playwright, party hack, and paid defamer.

Behind this cloud of poisoned ink some truth may hide. It seems, for example, that when Mrs. Manley enjoyed the Duchess's hospitality, Goodman was living in lodgings apart. His reason for keeping hidden his other mistress would be doubly valid if she was his wife. There is reason to suspect that he took a wife some time in 1690 or 1691, or that, at least, he lived with a woman whom he called "wife"—perhaps Mrs. Wilson, of the Pope's Head. I have found no record of Cardell's marriage, and it is possible that he never took the trouble to go through a legal ceremony. Obviously, so long as he was dependent upon the Duchess, he would keep the other woman a secret.

At least one of his fellow servants, George Marsh, knew about his "wife." At Sir John Fenwick's trial before the House of Lords in 1696, Marsh deposed that, one night three or four years earlier, he had found a convivial crew drinking healths, no doubt in Cardell's lodgings. Present were Goodman and his "wife," William O'Brian, Goodman's comrade in many a highway robbery, and one Mr. Lusay, or Lewsey, a Jacobite. Said Marsh, "I know Mr. Goodman, and he called himself God the Holy Ghost, the other[s] God the Father and God the Son, and drank such healths[!] and called to Lusay to stir the fire; and then one [O'Brian] said 'Here is the devil's health,' which Goodman drank, and called his wife the Virgin Mary." The blasphemy, which shocked the House of Lords, may have been Marsh's invention, but it is not inappropriate to the character of a libertine, "an Infidel profess'd."[19]

To turn from one extreme to another, in 1692 Charles Gildon, a budding poet, critic, and hack biographer, edited a volume of *Miscellany Poems upon Several Occasions,* a slim collection of verses by a number of mediocre poets. To it he prefixed an "Epistle Dedicatory to Mr. Cardell Goodman." Admitting the risk he ran of being considered "a servile, nauseous Sycophant" for praising a patron, Gildon wrote, "This Hazard, Sir, I must run, if I will declare in Public what I know of those excellent Accomplishments, which render you so dear to all that are acquainted with you. Your Wit and your Courage are things not to be question'd, much less your Generosity, that being a Vertue that never resides alone." Generosity, he said, was "the King of Vertues," and Goodman was "Generous almost to a fault." Gildon had reasons, he said, to "aver this, viz. my own Knowledg, and the Experience of several others." After a long digression on generosity, virtue, and the purpose of satire versus that of panegyric, he concluded with the hope that his little book would convey Goodman's name to posterity, "and with it the Testimony—how great a value I put upon your Worth, and how much I am, Sir, without reserve, Your humble Servant, Charles Gildon."

Between the extremes of libel and panegyric, truth hangs like Mahomet's coffin. It is unlikely that Cardell was as ugly, impotent, beggarly, boastful, pock-fret, and unscrupulous as the Court libelers and Mrs. Manley asserted in their desire to destroy the Duchess of Cleveland. On the other hand, seventeenth century dedications were almost always couched in terms of servile flattery; it is hard to believe that Cardell was truly distinguished for wit, courage, and generosity. However, dedicators usually crooked the pregnant hinges of the knee where thrift might follow fawning. Goodman resembled Shakespeare's Horatio in at least one respect: aside from what the Duchess gave him, he had no revenue save his good spirits to feed and clothe him. He had nothing with which to reward a mercenary dedicator.

On the whole, then, perhaps we should take Gildon's dedication at something near its face value: an expression of gratitude by an aspiring young writer whom Goodman had befriended and helped with a few shillings, some encouraging words, and perhaps an introduction to the playhouse. A man who could help young poets and encourage young actors like Colley Cibber could not have been completely bad.

VIII

To Kill a King

Cardell Goodman was a Jacobite. The term covered a multitude of Tories who favored, followed, or plotted for the return of King James the Second, since 1689 an exile with his wife and son at Saint Germain, just outside of Paris. Nonjuring clergymen who refused to swear allegiance to William and Mary because, they said, they had already sworn fealty to a still living king were called Jacobites, but most nonjurors were peaceful men who would rather pray than plot. Deluded Catholics who schemed and worked for the return of their royal co-religionist were certainly Jacobites, and so were those Protestants who forgot the follies of James, hated the rule of Dutch William, and longed for the good old days. Politicians who saw their places taken by Dutchmen sometimes played double roles, pretending loyalty to William and Mary, but secretly wooing King James with letters of fulsome compliment and empty promise. Some sober but short-sighted men, appalled at the cost of English blood and treasure in the long war with France (declared on May 7, 1689), wanted James back if only to end that war. Some men became Jacobites out of loyalty and misplaced love; some for money; others in hope of advancement and power; and many just for excitement and good company.

Robert Bruce, Earl of Ailesbury, was an excellent example of the Protestant peer who remained loyal to King James, even though, as a pragmatist, he recognized William and Mary as rulers de facto, and took an oath to that effect. A tall, stooped, dignified gentleman, he was high-minded, honorable, and more good-natured than prudent. He detested the Dutch, yearned for the return of James, and tried to keep out of foolish plots cooked up by the hot-headed and immature. In spite of his good intentions he became involved in Jacobite plots, with almost fatal results.

By contrast, in the dark pattern of Cardell Goodman's life no thread of gold blazons his commitment to a cause, good or bad. "An Infidel profess'd," he cared not a straw whether England was ruled by a Catholic or a Protestant. He was a Jacobite partly because of his education at the Tory stronghold of St. John's College, partly because conspiracy brought excitement into his aimless life, but chiefly becuase of his associations. Some of his playhouse friends had a kindness for King James, and at least two popular playwrights, Dryden and Wycherley, were "professed Jacobites." The actors had no reason to love William and Mary, who rarely came to the theatre and even more rarely commanded plays at Whitehall. (Of course William spent the better part of every year with his army in Flanders.) The tiring rooms of the theatres were convenient places for treasonable talk, and even for the singing of seditious ballads.

In 1693, for example, "Mrs. Lettice, a woman of the playhouse," was heard singing "a beastly Lampoone on the Queen." It seems that she had also been 'dispersing seditious Libells." Bridget Laytus, a mantua maker at the Theatre Royal, was arrested and tried at the Old Bailey on the charge of "Composing and Publishing 2 false and Seditious Libels, one called, A Song made upon the King, another, A Song made upon the Queen, the Burdens of which Songs were, *A dainty fine King, a dainty fine Queen, indeed, indeed.*" Mrs. Laytus protested "that she thought it was no harm to sing" the songs, but the Whig judges sentenced her to pay a fine of £200 and to stand once in the pillory at the May Pole in the Strand, and again in the pillory at Charing Cross.[1]

Goodman's most important association, of course, was with the Duchess of Cleveland, who had many reasons besides her avowed Catholicism to prefer gloomy James, who paid her pension, over sour William who neglected it. It seems, too, that Jacobitism was fashionable among "the Ladies at t'other end of Town"—in Mayfair, Piccadilly, and St. James's Square. The author of *The Character of a Jacobite* (1696) remarks, "The Women, I say, aiming at that Modish Name, Jacobite, enjoyn the

Beaus to do the like; and when they are in Company with 'em, will often start up this question, as, 'Well, Sir Novelty, Who are you for, King James or King William?' He having so much sense to know the Lady's for James, placing him first, crys, 'O Ged, Madam! I'm a Jacobite.' 'Ay, indeed, Sir,' says she, 'I'm o' your Mind; the Williamites are such slovenly Fellows.'—'O! Pox take 'em, Madam, nauseous Puppies, I loath the Name of 'em; I'm a true Jacobite. Stop my Vitals! King James has promised me a Colonels Commission to secure his throne for him, when he comes over.'"

This all sounds uncomfortably parallel to what Goodman's situation must have been with his mistress. True, when the leaders of the Jacobite conspiracy first drew him in, about 1694, they offered him only a captaincy, instead of a colonelcy, in a troop of horse to be raised for the conquest of England, but no doubt the Duchess encouraged him to accept the offer. The plotters also entrusted him with two boxes containing arms, which he in turn gave to the Duchess for safekeeping. Perhaps it was only make-believe and good fun to Cardell—the secret meetings, the boastful talk, the wild plans, the heavy drinking, and the songs. One pictures a swaggering lot of rakehells in a tavern raising their bumpers and roaring out a typical Jacobite song:

To our Monarchs return
Wee our glasses advance,
Whilst one is in Flanders
The other in France.

In this generous circle
I'm sure there are none,
But wish well to Kings,
And to each King his own.

Then here's to his health,
Lett him come lett him come boys
Send one into England
And both are at home boys.[2]

As long as the Jacobites confined themselves to peaceful demonstrations on the birthday of Prince James, "the pretended Prince of Wales" (June 10) and on the birthday of King James

(October 14), the authorities tended to ignore them. On Sunday, October 14, 1694, for instance, when "ye Jacobites appeared in yre utmost gaiety and had upon yre Cravatts an Embroydered Crowne with ye Letters J: K and one of ye healths they drank was to Turning in of ye Turnd out and yn a health to ye Turner," no one bothered them.

But the death of Queen Mary on December 28, 1694, cost William many supporters and emboldened the Jacobites. On the night of June 10, 1695, they lighted bonfires in many parts of town. One blazed merrily at the door of the Dog Tavern in Drury Lane where a club of Jacobites (among them, of course, "Mr. Goodman, the late player") celebrated the birthday of Prince James, "the warming-pan baby," with kettledrums, trumpets, and bumpers of wine. They insisted that every passerby drink to the health of King James and the titular Prince of Wales. When one doughty Whig drank instead to the health of King William and cried "Damnation to the sham Prince of Wales," a drunken Jacobite laid his head open with a sword. A mob gathered, seized arms and cobblestones, routed the roisterers, broke the tavern windows, and sacked the house. Finally the tavern keeper got rid of them by giving them money to buy drinks elsewhere.[3]

Riots could not be ignored. On July 3 a Grand Jury at Hick's Hall, acting on the information of a drawer at the Dog Tavern, found true bills for treason against twenty members of the Jacobite company. Some of these had criminal records; some were mere empty-headed idlers. Two men, Balthazar Redding and Mr. Pate, were singers employed at Betterton's recently opened playhouse in Lincolns Inn Fields. The Lord Chamberlain promptly ordered their dismissal. Two others, Thomas Rowe, the Duchess of Cleveland's solicitor, and one Mr. Williams, a surgeon, had left before the riot started. Sir John Fenwick, a famous malcontent and Jacobite leader who had once insulted Queen Mary by "cocking" his hat in her face, had been at the time of the riot "so drunk he could not stir, and yt he gave in evidence for himself when he was indicted."

Brought to trial, Rowe, Williams, and Fenwick were acquitted. Six of the rioters, chief among them Captain George Porter ("a monster of a man," said Ailesbury), were fined sums ranging from 100 to 500 marks (roughly £70 to £350). The others, including Goodman who surrendered on July 10, after weeks in hiding, gave bail and managed to get their cases removed from the Old Bailey to the Court of the King's Bench, thus postponing trial. Meanwhile, by combining bribery and threats, they got the tavern drawer, chief witness for the crown, "out of the way." Their cases were never tried.[4]

Accustomed as Cardell was to courts and prisons, this sort of thing was no longer fun, and from this time on he seems to have taken less interest in plots and conspiracies. Unfortunately, although he was never important in Jacobite councils, he had committed himself so deeply that, whether he withdrew or continued, he was bound to share the destiny of his fellows.

Behind the screen of cravats and bonfires, the fanatic Jacobites had long been pondering plans to kidnap King William as the prelude to an invasion by King James and a French army. In the spring of 1694 a group of madcaps led by Captain George Porter had met at Goodman's house in Brownlow (now Betterton) Street to discuss plans. The problem was what to do with William after they captured him. Should they shut him up in a fort at Deal? Should they ship him off to France? Goodman declared later that he flatly refused to "offer anything to his person," and one gathers that, at that time, few of the plotters seriously favored murder. In spite of the "legal" execution of King Charles the First, divinity still hedged a King. Nevertheless, Goodman had been one of the conspirators; he had later attended a meeting at which ways of furthering an invasion were discussed, and he had accepted King James's commission. Whether he had joined in the plot with serious intent, or merely to please his Jacobite mistress, or simply for excitement and adventure made no difference. He had plotted high treason, even though he had not committed it.

In 1696 the Jacobite plots came to a head. Early in the new year the Duke of Berwick, King James's natural son by Katherine Sedley, was seen skulking about London, whispering to known Jacobites in dark corners. Just as he set out for France by way of Romney Marsh, aided by the "owlers" (smugglers) who plied their illicit trade between the two warring countries, a score of soldiers in mufti slipped quietly into London. They were members of King James's guards, sent to England under the command of Sir George Barclay, a bigoted Scottish Catholic officer, to make war on King William.

Barclay planned to assassinate the King. Calculating that he needed at least forty men for the job, he got in touch with the extremist Jacobites who met almost daily at the Dog Tavern in Drury Lane or the King's Head in Leadenhall Street. Among them he found enough desperadoes to fill out his troop. Barclay knew that King William went every Saturday to Richmond to hunt, and that on his way back to his residence in Kensington Palace he always crossed the Thames by ferry near Turnham Green, taking coach again on the Middlesex side of the river. From the ferry led a narrow, muddy lane, ideal for an ambuscade. Barclay planned to fall on the coach from one side with eight or ten men armed with blunderbusses and musketoons. One party of horsemen commanded by Captain Porter and Mr. Robert Charnock was to assault the escort of half a dozen guards from the rear, and another party commanded by Brigadier Ambrose Rookwood was to attack from the front. The attempt was set for Saturday, February 15, 1696. If it succeeded, a light in Dover Tower was to be the signal for King James at Calais to embark with his French forces for the conquest of England.[5]

There are good reasons to believe that Cardell Goodman was not one of the Fearless Forty. We have the statement of Major John Bernardi, a relatively innocent victim of Parliamentary tyranny, that Goodman was never "so much as mentioned or charged with the Knowledge of, or of being in any Manner concerned in, the Assassination Plot." Moreover, Francis de la Rue, one of the Forty who turned King's evidence, deposed that while the final plans were being drawn he had asked Captain Porter "whether Goodman was concerned in this Business of murthering the King? because he was in last year's design" to kidnap him. Porter replied, "No, because he [Goodman] would not be contented without being made acquainted with the whole Scheme and Design thereof, therefore they did not communicate it to him, not thinking him easy to comply with their method, but would be troublesome in opposing their project, to make them comply with his Manner." In short, knowing that Goodman would not be a party to murder, the conspirators told him nothing.[6]

The plot was a masterpiece of simplicity, sure of success. But just before the fatal date, two Jacobites, Captains Richard Fisher and Thomas Pendergrasse, cursed with qualms of conscience, hurried to Whitehall with their stories. (Immediately thereafter Fisher disappeared and was never heard from again.) King William was persuaded to cancel his weekly trip. A third Jacobite, Francis de la Rue, added his evidence a few days later and gave a list of names. Acting on their combined evidence, the Secretary of State sent out messengers to seize the plotters, and the King issued a proclamation, giving their names and offering a reward of £1,000 for the arrest of each. Alarmed, fearful, and greedy, every citizen laid hands on the nearest suspicious person and called the watch. A few plotters, including Captain Barclay, managed to escape to France. The rest, taken in bed, dug out of cellars, recognized in spite of their disguises as beggars, clergymen, and even women, were swept up along with hundreds of innocent small fry and thrown into prison, while all available Jacobite peers were sent to the Tower. Newgate was crammed so full that the London militia—the trained bands—had to be called out to guard it.

On February 28 it was reported that "The Earle of Castlemayne [Barbara's husband] hath surrendered himself, and Goodman, the player, is in Newgate; who is his Duchess' favourite." In mortal terror the Duchess proclaimed that Goodman was no longer in her service and sent the two chests of arms in her keeping to a Jacobite friend, John Gisborne, telling him that they were filled with fine porcelain which he was to keep as a pledge for £150 she owed him. Later, when Gisborne's lodgings were searched, the arms were found, and he was imprisoned in the Gatehouse. On July 3 he petitioned to be granted at least the "liberty of the prison." He had been in solitary confinement for three months.[7]

To save his own neck, Captain Porter turned King's evidence and babbled everything he knew, betraying to his death even his own manservant, Thomas Keys, "a poor ignorant trumpeter who had his dependance on Porter," and acted under his master's orders. Other plotters tumbled over themselves in their haste to become evidences in their turn. Since Porter had been the ringleader in a number of abortive plots, he knew a great deal, and named not only commoners but peers. For the commoners justice was swift. On March 18 three of the conspirators, convicted on the evidence of Porter and his fellow turncoats, were drawn on sledges to the gallows, hanged until half dead, cut down, emasculated, disemboweled, beheaded, and quartered. Their heads were set up on London Bridge and their quarters on the city gates. Two more were executed on April 3, and three on April 29.[8]

The Whig ballad-writers, exulting over the failure of the plot, turned out a spate of bad verse. In *The Jacobites Lamentation and Confession*, 1696, one balladmonger wrote as if he were a Jacobite. One stanza goes thus:

> *The King was first to be Destroy'd*
> *By Poniard, Sword, or Gun,*
> *And we to give the French the Sign,*
> *When once that Work was done:*
> *The French were strait to land in Kent;*
> *In London then were we*
> *To Plunder, Burn, and Cut your Throats,*
> *For which, Boys, up go we.*

The Jacobite retorts were hollow. The best they could do was to claim, in *A New Ballad giving a true Account of the late horrid Conspiracy*, 1696, that King William himself engineered the plot as a device to get control of Parliament. He was represented as saying,

> *Full Sixty shall Join*
> *In a horrid Design*
> *Against our own Person and Crown,*
> *And then we will find*
> *Four amongst them so kind*
> *To make this Black Villainy known.*
>
> *In the Plot men of three*
> *Religions shall be,*
> *And the Scumm of Four Severall Nations.*
> *A Pretty Conceit*
> *English Ideots to cheat,*
> *Shall be join'd in one assassination.*

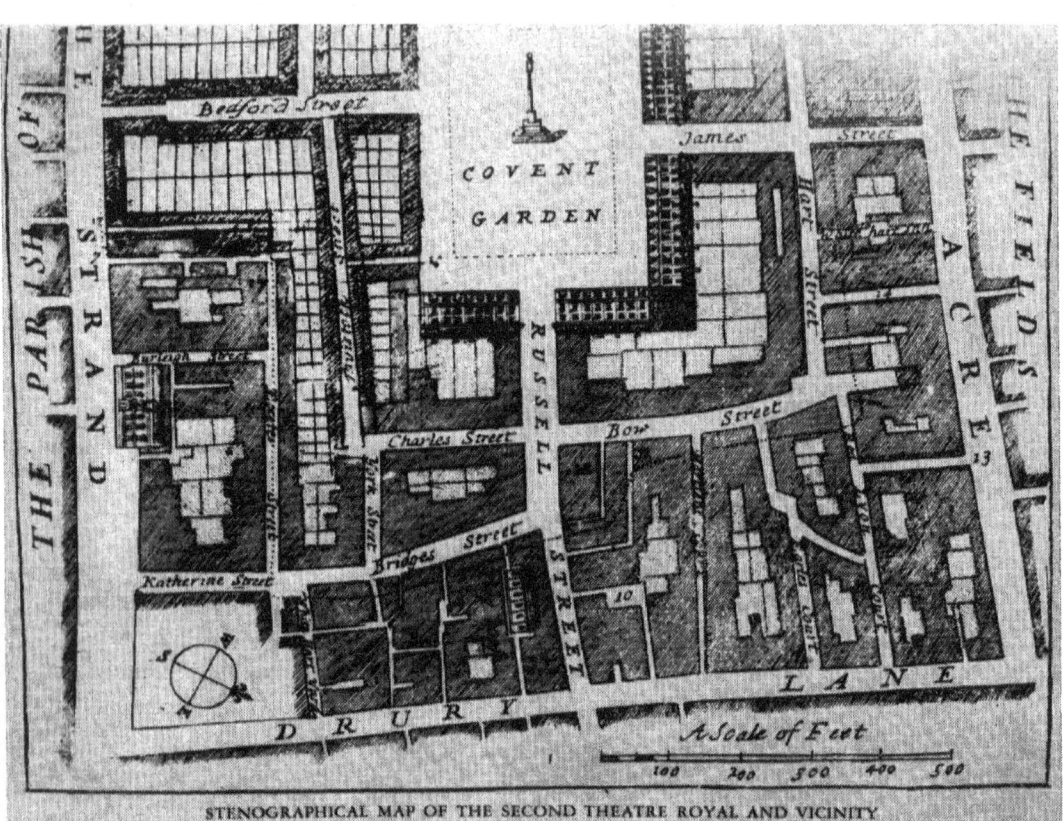

STENOGRAPHICAL MAP OF THE SECOND THEATRE ROYAL AND VICINITY
Strype's Stow, 1720

With eight conspirators executed, the government should have been content, but some powerful Whigs wanted the lives and properties of two Jacobite lords, the Earl of Ailesbury and Viscount Montgomery, and King William had a particular pique against Sir John Fenwick. Ailesbury was in the Tower; Montgomery and Fenwick were still at large. Although none of the three could be directly connected with the assassination plot, Captain Porter placed all of them at two meetings in the spring of 1695, when ways of furthering a French invasion had been discussed, and as a result Robert Charnock had been sent to France with a letter to King James. Mere presence at such meetings constituted high treason, but for conviction the Attorney General had to have two witnesses. Of those present at the meetings, three men—Charnock, Sir John Freind, and Sir William Perkins—had gone to their deaths on the scaffold with tight-sealed lips. Even Porter gave his evidence against Ailesbury with reluctance. In June, 1688, Porter had bought from the earl an annuity of £200, valid for the period of their joint lives. If he swore away Ailesbury's life, he would be so much the poorer.

After the executions only three men were left to testify to one or both of the two meetings: Captain Porter, Cardell Goodman, and young Peter Cooke, "a shatter-brained fellow." Cooke and Goodman were pressed to become crown witnesses. Cooke leaped at the chance to save his life, and poured out his little soul in a series of ill-written, misspelled, hysterical letters which completely mystified the Lords Justices, (the King's viceroys when William was fighting in Flanders). Facts and fables were hopelessly confused, and Cooke appeared so weak and dim-witted that the Attorney General feared to put him on the stand. Suddenly Cardell Goodman, ex-comedian, became an important political figure. The Lords Justices decided that they had to have his testimony; without it none of the three leading Jacobites could be convicted.

In Newgate Cardell had fallen sick, and now a physician, Sir Edmund King, was sent to minister to him. Archbishop Thomas Tenison, one of the Lords Justices, brought him spiritual comfort, reminded him of his sins, and promised a pardon if he turned King's evidence. Possibly the prelate and the player were already acquainted. Tenison, too, was a Cantabrigian, and all through the plague years had been vicar of St. Andrew the Great in Cambridge. Moreover, from 1680 to 1691 he had been rector of St. Martin's in the Fields, London, a church popular with actors. At any rate, he seems to have taken a kindly interest in the prisoner, perhaps because Cardell was the son of a deprived clergyman.

At first Cardell resisted the archbishop's persuasions, taking pride in playing out his *vilaine* role to the end. After several visits, Tenison played his trump card. "Master Goodman," he said sadly, "Peter Cooke hath discovered all, and you must hang or be hanged."[9]

Left in a cold, damp cell, without benefit of counsel, sick, and convinced that Cooke had "discovered all" about Goodman's part in the conspiracy, and that if he refused to testify against his friends he would certainly hang, Cardell broke down. No doubt he had been prepared to make a grandiose exit, to go to his death like the hero of any love-and-honor tragedy with firm steps, head high, and a rant upon his lips. But Cooke's accusation had reduced tragedy to a simple conflict between two equally guilty men, only one of whom need die.

In conversation with a fellow prisoner, one Edwards (alias Douglas), Cardell said resentfully, "He [Cooke] swore against me."

"How comes it then," said Edwards, "that he is not come off and has not a pardon?"

"He would give an account of nobody else but me," said Cardell, "and that was the reason he had no pardon. . . . He or I must suffer. But 'tis a foolish thing to be hang'd; all that is said of a man that is hang'd, is, that he hang'd handsomely, or he dy'd bravely."

Goodman cared nothing for Cooke—a worthless fellow. But he knew that he would have to bear witness against Fenwick, Ailesbury, and Montgomery, worthy men whom he respected. However, one could only live for the day and let the future take care of itself. Fenwick and Montgomery were still in hiding, and Ailesbury had powerful friends. Most of all, like every man, Cardell wanted to live. And what a way to die! To an actor who had imitated death so often and so gloriously upon the stage it was "a foolish thing to be hang'd," to mount a ladder with a rope around his neck and the hangman at his side, to be flung off and sway, half-strangled, until a swift hand cut the rope, and the Tyburn butchers went about their bloody business. Greater men than Goodman have broken under the terror of that fell sergeant, Death, but Cardell ("much against his will," said Ailesbury) "struck in" as an evidence not only because he wanted to live but also he saw death by hanging as "a foolish thing."[10]

On April 10, Cardell wrote to Archbishop Tenison,

My Lord,
I have all the reason imaginable to owne ye care yr Grace has of me, & ye concern that I find yr Lady has showne. I shall be ready to satisfy you in all I know and am recollecting & endeavouring to do wt service I can in recompense of yr favors.

I am my Lord

My humble duty	Yr Graces most humble &
& my poor wifes to	most obedient Servt[11]
yr Lady	

A week later Cardell was conveyed to Whitehall, severely questioned, and sent back to Newgate to continue "recollecting" for another week. On April 24, he gave James Vernon, one of the Secretaries, a full, detailed account of everything he remembered about the invasion plot. About the assassination plot he could say nothing. On April 28 he joined Captain Porter in giving evidence to a Grand Jury which brought in a true bill for high treason against Peter Cooke. In his testimony Goodman described a meeting at the King's Head Tavern in Leadenhall Street to discuss various invasion plans to be submitted to King James. (Ailesbury said of the same meeting, "In going out we met Mr. Goodman the player on the stairs.")

On May 13 Cooke was tried at the Old Bailey. Porter repeated the statement he had made to the Grand Jury. Then Goodman testified. "My Lord," he said, "About the middle of May last, or thereabouts, Captain Porter sent to me, and told me there was a Meeting of some Gentlemen of our acquaintance at the King's-Head in Leaden-Hall-street; and he desired me that I wou'd be there, because it was about business; I told him I did not know whether I cou'd be there at Dinner; but however, I wou'd not fail of coming thither after Dinner; and accordingly I came. When I came into the House, I sent up my Name to Captain Porter, and he came down and brought me up stairs, and there I saw my Lord Montgomery, my Lord of Aylesbury, Sir John Fenwick, Sir William Parkins, Sir John Freind, Mr. Charnock, and that Gentleman at the Barr, Mr. Cook . . ."

The lawyers for the defense concentrated their fire on Goodman, seeking to prove that as a man convicted of a crime he was not a valid witness. From the Records of the King's Bench they read the account of his conviction for conspiring with Alexander Amadei to poison the Dukes of Grafton and Northumberland. Their arguments were brushed aside by the court because, as Chief Justice Treby said in his summing up, "the Government was convinc'd that he was wrong'd by a causeless Prosecution, and the Evidence against him was found not to be credible. And besides, Mr. Goodman stands pardoned by several Acts of Pardon [specific and general], as well as other Subjects."

Fighting for a lost cause, the defense lawyers brought in the owner and the drawers of the King's Head, who swore that they did not see Goodman at the tavern on the day in question. But their statements were dismissed as inconclusive. In fine, the jury found Cooke guilty of high treason. Hoping that his evidence might yet be useful, the Lords Justices reprieved him again and again and eventually procured his pardon because, as they said in a remarkable fit of sanity, "considering Mr. Cooke as a very weak man," they saw nothing to be gained by hanging him. A year after his conviction he was banished for life.[12]

There were those who maintained that Goodman lied under oath; and perhaps he did not tell the literal truth. There is no doubt that the meeting which he described took place, and that all those named by him and Captain Porter were present. But, if Ailesbury is to be believed, Goodman did not arrive until the meeting was over. Yet in his sworn deposition and on the witness stand he gave a circumstantial account of the meeting as if he had been present throughout. Very likely the Attorney General told him what to say; certainly his story was suspiciously like Porter's even to minute details. The threat of the gallows can stretch any man's conscience.

All through May, Goodman fretted in Newgate. The Lords Justices treated him with kindness, sent Nicholas Baker, a clerk, to help him "in the management of his private concerns, since it is not thought fit to give him his liberty," and on May 26 told Mr. James Fell, the Keeper of Newgate, "that it should not be looked upon as an offense, if Mr. Goodman went some times abroad to look after his private concerns provided he were still in his [Fell's] custody & under his eye." Clearly they meant to keep their hands on Goodman until he had given evidence against their three important victims. Meantime Cardell's fellow evidences were kept in luxury. De la Rue was living in richly furnished apartments in Whitehall, and Captains Porter and Pendergrass had a well appointed house near the palace, with everything paid for by the King.[13]

Near the end of May Cardell wrote plaintively to Archbishop Tenison,

Sr

I am in ye same unfortunate circumstances as to my liberty (notwithstanding my hopes) for Mr. ffell does not think himself safe wth a verball order and so I am left where I was. I beg of yr Grace a redress in this melancholy affaire for my confinement is my utter ruine. I am willing to give in Bayle & if I may be with a messenger I am content or any way yor Lordship with ye rest of the Lords Justices shall thinke fitt. For otherwayes wth want of money & want of health I shall perish here. I beg your Graces pardon for this trouble but I have noe friend to addresse to butt yr Grace for all ye rest of the world have turn'd their backs upon me."

Unfortunately for Cardell most of his friends were also suspected as Jacobites. For example, among those in the custody of messengers on April 24, 1696, were William O'Brian, Balthazar Redding, and Mr. Lewsay. However, Tenison pleaded Cardell's cause to good effect. Probably the Lords Justices were moved also by the fact that on May 29 Porter and Goodman testified before a Grand Jury which brought in true bills against Fenwick and Montgomery. On June 5 the Justices signed an order "for the bailing of Goodman" and three lesser witnesses, Hunt, Boyce, and Blair.[14]

On June 9, after three months in Newgate, Cardell was out on bail. (Fenwick was captured the next day.) Cardell was freed to go about London as he chose, but unlike other evidences who had been fully pardoned, he remained in the shadow of the gallows. The Lords Justices had learned a lesson early in May when Fenwick's family tried to bribe Porter to abscond. Two Irishmen, acting as go-betweens, offered him three hundred guineas in hand, another three hundred as soon as he was out of the country, a pension of £200 a year, a pardon from King James, and a safe refuge in France. Anticipating a still larger reward from the English government, Porter betrayed the Irishmen, who were fined and pilloried. (Porter was allowed to keep the three hundred guineas.) Goodman, a reluctant witness, was a player—and therefore the more easily bribed![15]

In spite of his complaints, Goodman did not entirely lack friends. He seems to have returned to his old haunts, including the theatres, but not to his former post with the Duchess of Cleveland. Whatever her feelings about him may have been, she dared not admit him, even secretly, to her house. Although her pension was for life, its payment depended on the good will of King William's government, and Goodman was well watched by Matthew Smith and John Robins, informers paid by the Secretary of State. Any contact between Cardell and the Duchess could bring her loyalty into question.

No one seems to have thought the worse of Cardell for trying to save his own life. It was the way of the world, and he was only one of a dozen Jacobites who found it easier to confess than be hanged. At least he was not as bad as Captain Porter, who was hated by Jacobites and Williamites alike. Perhaps it was a disgusted Jacobite who wrote a short libel call "On P[orter] the E[vidence],"

> *When God to punish Adams sons inclin'd*
> *From fire and brimstone Judas saved Mankind:*
> *And P[orter] by a pious treachery*
> *Preserv'd his King and set his Country free.*
> *Both did but in a different sphere trepan,*
> *The one hang'd his Master the other his Man.*
> *If for this deed P[orter's] so highly priz'd,*
> *By God I'le have Iscariot Cannoniz'd.*[16]

Some time during the summer of 1696, when Goodman "was expected to be an Evidence against Sir John Fenwick," young Colley Cibber met the former player at the house of Sir Thomas Skipwith, one the Theatre Royal patentees. Cardell may have had a more than merely social reason for dining with Skipwith. Since April, 1695, when Betterton, Elizabeth Barry, Anne Bracegirdle, and a number of other malcontent players deserted the Theatre Royal and started acting in the old Lincolns Inn theatre, there had been two companies again. Now the King's Company was badly in need of competent players, and Cardell was out of a job. Skipwith (said Colley) "as he was an agreeable Companion himself, liked Goodman for the same quality." At forty-three Cardell was a pleasant fellow, a good raconteur with a flippant style, living for the moment with all the carelessness of the true hedonist.

However confused Colley's recollection of the facts brought out in conversation after dinner, when Cardell "without disguise or sparing himself, fell into a laughing account of several loose Passages of his younger Life," there is no mistaking the airy tone. For his exploits on the highway years ago, Cardell said, "King James was prevail'd upon to pardon him." King James's pardon was really for Goodman's supposed attempt to poison the two young dukes, but, of course, it blanketed all antecedent crimes. This kindness, Cardell continued, "was doing him so particular an Honour that no Man could wonder if his Acknowledgement had carried him a little farther than ordinary into the interests of that Prince; But as he had lately been out of luck in backing his old Master, he had now no way to get home the Life he was out upon his Account but by being under the same obligation to King William." To Cardell, all the world was still a stage, and he would play his debonaire role to the end.[17]

Summer went by, and Sir John Fenwick was told to prepare for trial. His solicitor, Mr. Christopher Dighton, tried every possible device to save his client's life. Afraid to approach either Porter or Goodman in person lest he suffer the fate of the two Irish suborners, Dighton sought out Thomas Rowe, the Duchess of Cleveland's agent.

"You know Goodman well," said Dighton, "and if you can say anything that will discredit Goodman's testimony, you shall have £100 a year settled on you for life. Did you never hear him talk of poisoning the Duke of N[orthumberland] and robbing on the highway, and that he is concerned with clippers?"

"I have heard him talk of these matters several times," Rowe replied, "but you cannot think I will be a witness and expose myself and disparage people till I know for what."

"For that you shall be satisfied," said Dighton. "You shall have £100 a year settled upon you provided you can discredit Goodman's testimony, that Sir John Fenwick may come off, and it will be done by a friend of yours."

Rowe promised nothing. Instead he told Goodman what the solicitor had offered, and the two trotted dutifully to Whitehall to tell Archbishop Tenison. Goodman was faithful, in his fashion.[18]

By the device of accusing men high in the King's counsels, Fenwick got his trial postponed, first to September, and then to October. Finally Lady Mary Fenwick, "a great intriguer," who had once been pilloried as Lady Addleplot in D'Urfey's *The Boarding School* (1690), tried bribery again. She and Lady Montgomery (whose husband was still at large) put up the cash. Lord Ailesbury, asked to pay one-third, indignantly refused. He was secure in the consciousness of his own innocence. The two ladies chose one Major Robert Ingram as their messenger. Ingram found Goodman at the Dog Tavern and put his proposition bluntly. Claiming to represent Lords Ailesbury and Montgomery, he offered the former player £500 in hand and a pension of £500 a year to abscond to France. Everything for his flight would be arranged, including a ship to carry him across the Channel. To a broken, jobless man, this was a tempting offer. In France, where prices were low, he could live like a lord on £500 a year. Besides there was always the chance that King James or his son would ascend the English throne, and Goodman could return with honor, perhaps even ennobled by the exiled King!

Cardell went to talk things over with his old friend and fellow Jacobite, William O'Brian, once a corporal in the Blues. As Ailesbury tells the story (based, he says, on information secured later from a trusted friend), Cardell explained Ingram's proposition in detail, concluding, "I am a most unfortunate man. I must either be hang'd, or I must take away the lives of two innocent lords against whom I know nothing, nor of the least crime they have committed."

"Dear Goodman," said O'Brian, "if that be your case, why do you not accept the offer?"

"I am willing," said Goodman, "but I will not go away without you."

"I have no merit," O'Brian protested, "nor known to any of the Court of St. Germain. I half starve here, and there I should perish."

"In a word," said Goodman, "I will not go without you."

In a word, O'Brian agreed. The two men made their preparations for flight in secret, telling only their wives. Paid in banknotes, which he discounted hurriedly at a loss, Goodman had plenty of money, and his way was smoothed by Major Ingram's underground. The fact that Cardell forfeited his bail, at the expense of some good friends, does not seem to have bothered him.

On the morning of October 29, Goodman and O'Brian took the Ipswich coach at the Cross Keys Inn in Gracechurch Street. At Ipswich they took another coach to a ferry near the coast, where a ship commanded by Joseph Saunders, an owler, awaited them. They had a long start. In London, Mrs. Goodman put off enquiries about her husband by "pretending every day she expected him home by night, and that he kept out of the way for avoiding duns." By the time his escape was discovered, he was safe in Calais.[19]

IX

The Epilogue

On November 5, 1696, King William issued a proclamation offering £1,000 reward for the apprehension of Cardell Goodman, who, "intending to Suppress the Information which he hath formerly given, and to prevent the further Prosecution of . . . Traytors . . . has lately Absconded from his usual Place of Abode, and is fled from Justice." But Cardell was safe in the sheltering arms of France.

Deprived of Goodman's evidence, the Whigs could not bring Fenwick to a criminal trial and were forced to fall back, for the last time in English history, upon the device of a bill of attainder in Parliament. Hearings on the bill were long and acrimonious, lasting from November 16 to December 23. In both Houses Porter gave his usual evidence, and Rowe testified to Dighton's attempt to get him to discredit Goodman. The Houses heard Goodman's depositions read, and examined members of the Grand jury as to the burden of his testimony before that body. In the House of Commons the defense brought up again the charge that Goodman had conspired to poison the Dukes of Grafton and Northumberland. In the House of Lords the defense brought in three new witnesses: Anne Cross and Edmond Godfrey, who deposed that Goodman had robbed them on the highway, and George Marsh, who testified to Goodman's wicked ways and blasphemous talk.

But Fenwick's cause was hopeless from the first. A powerful coalition of Whigs and Tories wanted his life—the Whigs because he had long been a dangerous Jacobite, the Tories because he knew too much and had exposed too many secrets. The bill would have passed without Goodman's testimony. One contemporary commented: "Goodman's evidence was not much insisted on. It was proved that he had been a common Highwayman; a Record was brought of designing to murder two of the Duchess of Cleveland's Sons; besides most horrid Blasphemies, that could scarce be heard with Patience." In the House of Commons the attainder bill passed with a majority of thirty-three; in the House of Lords with a majority of seven. On January 28, 1697, Sir John Fenwick was beheaded on Tower Hill.[1]

Fenwick was the last Jacobite to be executed as a result of the Assassination Plot, which, by an accident of history, is often called after him instead of after its real author, Sir George Barclay. Lord Ailesbury, freed from the Tower in February, 1697, fled to the Continent and spent the remainder of his long life in exile. Viscount Montgomery, who surrendered in December, 1696, was confined in Newgate until the following June. Freed on bail, without a trial, he too fled abroad. Capt. Pendergrasse was knighted and pensioned by King William. He fell at the Battle of Malplaquet. Francis de la Rue was killed in a vulgar tavern brawl. Peter Cooke died miserably ten years after his banishment. George Porter lived until 1728, but (says Ailesbury) "no honest man would speak to him," and he was to the last "despised and abhorred by all." Successive acts of Parliament kept Major Bernardi and four fellow Jacobites in Newgate without trial for the rest of their natural lives. Bernardi died in prison on September 20, 1736.[2]

In the closing years of the century all sorts of rumors about Goodman filtered back from France. Several correspondents wrote that he was "closely confined in a dungeon," or that "the French King has caused Goodman to be committed to the Bastille and put into irons, designing to break him upon the wheel for what he swore against Sir John Fenwick." The fact is that after a short sojourn in Calais, where some honest Frenchmen were incensed that he could walk the streets openly, Goodman went with O'Brian to Saint Germain. There they were "well received," but found nothing to interest them in the poverty-stricken, priest-ridden court of King James, who was very busy saving his own soul. Presumably the wives of the two fugitives joined them at Saint Germain, where a little colony of refugees eked out a narrow living on the charity of the exiled Queen. The only record we have of Goodman's life at Saint Germain is an entry in the parochial registers showing that "Cardell Goodman, gent., angl." was godfather at the baptism of Denis, infant son of Hugues Rourke and his wife Heleine. This was a decidedly new role for Alexander the Great.[3]

When his cash was all spent, and the money promised him as a pension failed to arrive from England, Goodman, dissatisfied, looked about for a new world to conquer. After the Treaty of Ryswick was signed on September 10, 1697, England and France resumed diplomatic relations. Goodman longed for his native soil and the taverns of Covent Garden. In January, 1698, William Bentinck, Earl of Portland, sailed for France as Ambassador, with the poet Matthew Prior as his secretary. Among his many instructions, Portland was charged with the duty of finding out and harrying the expatriates who had been in various Jacobite plots. But the Jacobites in France had too much to lose by giving up Goodman, who, under pressure, might expose some of the best English agents.

On January 19, 1698, the Earl of Middleton, King James's Secretary of State, wrote to King Louis' Foreign Secretary, the Marquis de Torcy, suggesting that Goodman, "who had been an evidence against several in England; and particularly had informed against the Duke of Powis [Lord Montgomery], who, however, bribed him to retire to France," should be sent to a place of safety. Middleton, aware that Cardell was "impatient" to return to England, feared that he might seek Lord Portland's protection. That spring it was rumored in England that "the French King hath delivered up Goodman," that "Goodman was imprisoned for talking too loosely of His Most Christian Majesty for having deserted his ally King James and made the peace," and that "There having been no talk of Goodman for a considerable time, some are of opinion that the World will hear no more of his evidence." For once opinion was correct.[4]

After 1698 the facts are obscured by the mists of time and distance. It appears that Goodman was arrested and sent to Dauphiné in southeastern France. Some months later his wife petitioned former Queen Mary for permission to join him. The chances are that her petition was granted. The French government and the exiled Queen had no reason to punish Goodman; they merely wished to keep him safe from English eyes.[5]

In this design they were not entirely successful. Lord Ailesbury was told by "the Countess of Salisbury that loved travelling, that as she passed in a felouque by Nice, under a fort in the French territories, she heard Goodman calling on them in English and naming himself unfortunate." Said Ailesbury, "I guess he perceived the felouque had English on board." The countess who loved travelling was Frances, widow of James Cecil, fourth Earl of Salisbury. From June to September 1699 she lingered in Paris, en route to Rome for the Jubilee. Probably she saw Goodman that autumn on her way to Rome. For the remaining years of the Truce of Ryswick, Goodman's voice was heard no more in the land, and the outbreak of the War of the Spanish Succession, in May, 1702, dropped a blazing curtain between England and France.[6]

Meanwhile, in Brussels, the kindly Earl of Ailesbury, hearing that O'Brian and his wife were starving at Saint Germain, offered him a job as his secretary. On his arrival to take up his duties, English agents arrested O'Brian (illegally, of course) and sent him to England. He was quickly freed and sent back to Brussels, but he proved to be so overbearing and troublesome that after eighteen months Ailesbury discharged him. O'Brian went to Paris and became a captain in the Duke of Berwick's regiment.[7]

By this time all but the most dogged Jacobites had given up hope of a restoration. The Act of Settlement (June, 1701), which limited the monarchical succession to the heirs of Electress Sophia after William and Princess Anne (if both died childless), was a severe blow. Then on September 5, 1701, when King James the Second died in the odor of sanctity, and King Louis promptly recognized his son James, "the Old Pretender," as King of England, the Jacobites revived. On February 21, 1702, King William's horse, Sorrel, which had once belonged to Sir John Fenwick, stumbled over a molehill and threw the King, whose collarbone was broken. Two weeks later William died, in his fifty-second year. The ecstatic Jacobites celebrated William's death with toasts to "the little gentleman in black velvet" whose burrowing had caused it, and eulogized Sorrel as an

> *Illustrious steed who should the Zodiac grace,*
> *To whom the Lyon and the Bull give place.*
> *Blest be the duggs that fed thee, blest the Earth*
> *Which first received thee, and beheld thy birth.*

But in slow, deliberate majesty, Good Queen Anne ascended the English throne.[8]

From 1696 to 1705, Barbara, Duchess of Cleveland, lived in quiet obscurity. If she found a replacement for Cardell Goodman, no gossip or Court libeler noted the fact. She had lost one son, the rough Duke of Grafton, who was killed at the siege of Cork in 1692, but she still had two sons, three daughters, several grandchildren—and a husband.

On July 21, 1705, the Earl of Castlemaine died. Although the newly-widowed Duchess was then sixty-four, she was still comely, and her pension of £100 a week out of the Post Office made her a tempting prize. The vultures gathered. Eminent among them was Major-General Robert Fielding, a middle-aged gamester and sharper, commonly called "Handsome" Fielding. This irresistible rogue had two wealthy widows in view at the same time: the Duchess and young Mrs. Anne Deleau, whose merchant husband had left her a fortune of £60,000. On November 5, 1705, Fielding secretly wedded and bedded Mrs. Deleau—or so he thought. Three weeks later he persuaded the Duchess of Cleveland that he was just as manly as King Charles the Second or Alexander the Great. He married her privately on November 25.

For nearly a year Fielding managed to keep his bigamy a secret. In the meantime, however, he showed his true colors to the Duchess, treating her with coarse brutality and taking all the money he could lay his hands on. It was reported that he locked her up for several days "in a close roome, beateing & allmost starving her," that he "broak open her clossett doar and toock fower hundred pd. out," and that "he beat her sadly and she cryed out murder in the street out of the window, and he shott a blunderbuss at the people." When her sons came to Barbara's defense, Fielding threatened to kill them. Finally, on July 24,

THE EPILOGUE   133

1706, the Duchess described to Chief Justice Holt "the hard Usage and Threats she had receiv'd from her Husband, and being in danger of her life from him, Swore the Peace against him." Fielding, unable to post £2,000 bail, "& being also very insolent to his Lordship," the Chief Justice, was committed to Newgate.⁹

Of course all this scandal again focused the attention of gossips and libelers on the Duchess. One satirist made capital of the situation with *The Dutchess of C[leveland]'s Memorial. To the Tune of, The Dame of Honour*, which told the story of Barbara's many loves in scatological detail. The first two of seven stanzas will serve as a sample:

> *What tho' my Name is toss'd about,*
>   *For quarrelling with Beau F[ieldi]ng,*
> *As if I did begin to Doat,*
>   *And were to Duty yielding:*
> *Since I have him to Newgate sent,*
>   *To shew it was my Manner,*
> *No single Man could me content,*
>   *Since I was a Strump of Honour.*
>
> *I had an harmless wealthy Spouse,*
>   *Whose Name was R-g-r Pal—r,*
> *And decently did plant his Brows,*
>   *With Horns in ample manner.*
> *I, from his Arms to Rowley fled,*
>   *My Cole-black lovely Charmer,*
> *Then jumping into Royal Bed,*
>   *Was dubb'd a Whore of Honour.*

The satirist was not well informed. Of all Barbara's lovers after "Rowley" (King Charles) he mentioned only "'Fleshly Will [Wycherley]," "Jacob Hall that Cap'er[er] rare," and "scum Goodman." After all, most of her affairs were long past and forgotten. But Fielding was very much in the present. In *General Fielding's Answer to the Dutchess of C[leveland]'s Memorial*, the same versifier represented Fielding as saying,

> *If I was by misfortune sent,*
>   *To Newgate in a huff Sir,*
> *Yet I got out by free Consent,*

> *And stood both Kick and Cuff Sir,*
> *And as for those mean Sons of W—rs,*
> *That all my Glory grutches,*
> *I'll live to pay off all their Scores,*
> *And still defend my Dutchess.*

After two days in Newgate, Fielding found friends to go his bail. He returned to the Duchess's house only to find that she had moved out. Thereupon he had the impudence to publish an advertisement to the effect that his wife had left her husband's house near Piccadilly, taking with her goods and chattels belonging to the said husband, "worth about £3,000," and had since refused to return, saying that "she had put herself under the protection of her Children." Solemnly Fielding gave due notice "to all tradesmen and others, upon no Account whatsoever to Trust, or give Credit, to the said Duchess, whose Debts he will in no wise satisfy!" Ironically, on October 5, Fielding himself was arrested for debts "amounting to near fifteen hundred pounds."[10]

By this time Fielding's other wife, whom he had also mistreated, decided that she had had enough. She turned out to be, not Anne Deleau the fortune, but Mary Wadsworth, a woman of the town, who, with the aid of a scheming hairdresser, Charlotte Villars, had gulled Fielding into marrying her as Mrs. Deleau. Mary Wadsorth took her story to the young Duke of Grafton, Barbara's grandson.

On December 6, 1706, Fielding was convicted of bigamy. He pleaded his clergy, and the court was obliged to reduce the usual sentence of death for a felony to "burning in the hand." But he had also a warrant from Queen Anne to suspend execution of even that mild punishment, and therefore escaped scot-free. The Duchess sued for an annullment, and, on May 23, 1707, the Court of the Arches declared her marriage to Fielding void. Fielding acknowledged Mary Wadsworth as his wife and lived with her peaceably until his death, on May 12, 1712. The Duchess of Cleveland, perhaps unable to bear the laughter of the Town, retired to a house in Chiswick, where she died "of a dropsy," on October 9, 1709.[11]

Although Theophilus Lucas claims that Goodman "died of a Fever" in France "in the 50th year of his Age, Anno 1699," it seems that, in fact, the indestructible player survived his famous mistress. In his *Memoirs* (written 1728–32) Lord Ailesbury wrote of Goodman, "the last time I heard of him was by that unfortunate Mr. Forrester, that laid hands on himself." The Mr. Forrester who later committed suicide was "governor"—i.e., tutor—to young Thomas Grosvenor, second son of Sir Thomas Grosvenor, Bart., of Eaton in Cheshire. Making the grand tour of Europe within a year or two after the end of the war, in 1713, Grosvenor and his tutor met Goodman by accident while they were traveling through France. "Passing by Monteliman, a walled town between Lyons and Avignon, the inn-keeper told them that there was an English lord there, and they being curious to see his lordship," the landlord arranged a meeting with Goodman, and the two travelers "soon found out the mistake." Evidently Goodman was a resident of Monteliman perforce, confined to its boundaries. The French authorities allowed him "about a hundred pistoles [£87 10s] per year for his maintenance."

"Mr. Forrester told me many things that were favourable on his side," said Ailesbury, "but really I have forgotten them. He began to study well but preferred a stage life and excelled there, and although he was forced to be a witness, as hinted at before, the man had great remorse, and the worse thing I know of him was that he entered into that horrid conspiracy which brought on him his ruin."[12]

Let that be his epitaph.

Notes

References Frequently Cited

Ailesbury. *Memoirs of Thomas Earl of Ailesbury*, 2 vols., 1890.
Boswell. Eleanore Boswell, *The Restoration Court Stage (1660–1702)*, 1932.
Bulstrode. *The Bulstrode Papers . . . Newsletters Written to Sir Richard Bulstrode . . . 1673–1675*, 1896.
Cartwright. Julia Cartwright, *Sacharissa*, 1893.
Choyce Collection. "A Choyce Collection," MS miscellany, The Ohio State University Library.
Cibber. *An Apology for the Life of Mr. Colley Cibber*, ed. R. W. Lowe, 2 vols., 1889.
CSPD. *Calendars of State Papers, Domestic Series.*
CTB. *Calendars of Treasury Books.*
Davies. Thomas Davies, *Dramatic Miscellanies*, 3 vols., 1784.
Downes. John Downes, *Roscius Anglicanus* (1708), ed. Montague Summers, 1928.
Evelyn. *The Diary of John Evelyn*, ed. Henry B. Wheatley, 4 vols., 1906.
Fitzgerald. Percy Fitzgerald, *A New History of the English Stage*, 2 vols., 1882.
Gardner. *The Prologues and Epilogues of John Dryden*, ed. W. B. Gardner, 1951.
HMC. Appendices to the Reports of the Royal Commission on Historical Manuscripts.
Hooke. *The Diary of Robert Hooke, 1672–80*, ed. H. W. Robinson and W. Adams, 1935.
Hotson. Leslie Hotson, *The Commonwealth and Restoration Stage*, 1928.
Langbaine. Gerard Langbaine, *An Account of the English Dramatick Poets*, 1691.

L.C. Lord Chamberlain's Records, Public Record Office, London.
Lucas. Theophilus Lucas, *Lives of the Gamesters*, 1714.
Luttrell, Narcissus. *A Brief Relation of State Affairs*, 6 vols., 1857.
Newdigate. Newsletters addressed to Sir Richard Newdigate, The Folger Shakespeare Library, Washington, D. C.
Nicoll. Allardyce Nicoll, *A History of Restoration Drama*, 4th ed., 1952.
Pepys. *The Diary of Samuel Pepys*, ed. Henry B. Wheatley, 9 vols., 1893.
Portledge. *The Portledge Papers*, ed. R. J. Kerr & I. C. Duncan, 1928.
P.R.O. The Public Record Office, London.
Sergeant. Philip W. Sergeant, *My Lady Castlemaine*, 1911.
S.P. State Papers. Public Record Office, London.
State Trials. *Cobbett's Collection of State Trials*, ed. James Howell, Vols. XII, XIV, 1809.
Vernon. James Vernon, *Letters Illustrative of the Reign of William III*, 3 vols., 1841.
Ward. *The Letters of John Dryden*, ed. C. E. Ward, 1942.
Wiley. *Rare Prologues and Epilogues: 1642–1700*, ed. Autrey Nell Wiley, 1940.
Williamson. *Letters Addressed from London to Sir Joseph Williamson*, ed. W. D. Christie, 2 vols., 1874.
Wilson. John Harold Wilson, *All the King's Ladies*, 1958.
Wood. *The Life and Times of Anthony Wood*, ed. Andrew Clark, 5 vols., 1900.

I. Study to Stage pages 1–12

1. Lucas, p. 267; Capt. Alexander Smith, *The School of Venus*, 1716, II, 17.
2. Betterton's *History of the English Stage*, 1741, p. 110.
3. Thomas Macaulay, *The History of England*, 1849, VIII, 33.
4. Lucas, p. 260; Victoria County Histories, *Hertford*, 1902, III, 266–8, 389; Joseph Foster, *Alumni Oxonienses*; J. & J. A. Venn, *Alumni Cantabrigienses*; John Walker, *Sufferings of the Clergy during the Great Rebellion, 1642–60* (1714), ed. A. G. Matthews, 1948, p. 183; John Albin, *History of the Isle of Wight*, 1795, pp. 651–2. Mr. Goodman's verses are to be found in Lambeth MS. 937/19, Lambeth Palace Library. They have been recently published under a second title, *Beawty in Raggs*, edited by R. J. Roberts, University of Reading, 1958.
5. *CSPD*, 1650, p. 486; *CSPD*, 1651, pp. 32, 66, 93.
6. *The Diary of Samuel Newton*, ed. J. E. Foster, 1890, pp. 1, 12, 15.

7. Venn, *Alumni Cantabrigienses;* Montague Summers, *The Playhouse of Pepys,* 1935, pp. 434–6; Jane Lane, *Titus Oates,* 1949, pp. 22–4; Adam Elliott, *A Modest Vindication of Titus Oates,* 1682.

8. Ailesbury, II, 399. I am grateful to Mr. F. P. White, Keeper of the Records, St. John's College, for this item about Goodman's scholarship.

9. *The Diary of Samuel Newton,* pp. 43, 57, 58, 64; Additional MS. 36,916, f. 232; *Bulstrode,* I, 206; C. H. Cooper, *Annals of Cambridge,* 1845, III, 517–48.

10. Wood, III, 95–6.

11. Pepys, Nov. 14, 1666, April 7, 29, 1668; *Despatches of William Perwich,* ed. N. B. Curran, 1903, p. 116; James Howard's *The Man of Newmarket,* 1678, Act III, 1.

12. Cibber, II, 63–4.

13. L.C. 5/140, p. 139.

14. Lucas, pp. 260–66.

15. Hooke, pp. 9, 15, 36, 42, 52, 57, 109, 131, 370, 416.

II. The King's Company pages 13–32

1. Nicoll, pp. 284–320; Additional MS. 36,916, f. 233.

2. HMC. *Second Report,* p. 22; Hotson, p. 253; Epilogue to Shipman's *Henry the Third of France,* 1672.

3. Langbaine, p. 216; Gardner, p. 211.

4. Hotson, p. 348; Downes, p. 32; Prologue to Dryden's *The Assignation,* 1672.

5. Langbaine, p. 213; Gardner, p. 41; *Covent Garden Drollery* (1672), ed. George Thorn-Drury, 1928, pp. 1–5.

6. The players' petition is wrongly catalogued in *CSPD,* 1666, p. 299. For the warrants see L.C. 5/140, pp. 473–4, and Boswell, p. 296.

7. Hotson, p. 254; Nicoll, p. 323; *N&Q,* 5th Series, V (May 15, 1875), 385; 8th Series, X (July 4, 1896), 7, 58, 299; *Transactions of the Royal Historical Society,* Vol. X; Fitzgerald, I, 138–9.

8. Dryden, Preface to *The Assignation,* 1672; Nicoll, p. 347; *Bulstrode,* I, 254.

9. Boswell, pp. 117–18; Sybil Rosenfeld, *Foreign Theatrical Companies in Great Britain,* 1955, pp. 2–3; Gardner, p. 42; J. H. Wilson, "A Theatre in York House," *Theatre Notebook,* XVI, 3 (Spring, 1962), 75–8.

10. Hooke, p. 42; Evelyn, May 29, 1673.

11. Dennis, *Remarks upon Pope's Homer,* 1717; Dedication to *The*

NOTES 139

Empress of Morocco; L.C. 3/27, p. 94; *A Narrative, Written by E. Settle,* 1683; Boswell, pp. 131–33.

12. George Speaight, "The Earliest Known English Playbill," *Theatre Notebook,* VI (1951–2), pp. 34–5.

13. Hotson, p. 35; Wright, *Historia Histrionica,* printed in Cibber, I, xxiv–v; for Haines see Pepys, March 7, 1668; for Leigh and Griffin see L.C. 5/14, p. 96. Both were arrested with others for showing plays in London without license.

14. Downes, p. 35; Hotson, pp. 190–2.

15. See L.C. 3/26, p. 209; L.C. 3/27, pp. 96, 97; L.C. 3/28, p. 201; Nicoll, p. 324.

16. See L.C. 5/143, p. 69.

17. Nicoll, p. 324. The oath is given in full in L.C. 5/137, p. 1. See also L.C. 5/41, f. 17; L.C. 3/61, p. 65.

18. Dennis, *The Character and Conduct of Sir John Edgar,* 1720.

19. H. B. Wheatley, *London Past and Present,* 1891, III, 99; Pepys, Feb. 3, 1664, Jan. 24, 1669.

20. *CSPD,* 1671, p. 271; Additional MS. 32,362, f. 19.

21. W. J. Lawrence, "Oxford Restoration Prologues," *TLS,* Jan. 16, 1930; Sybil Rosenfeld, "Some Notes on the Players in Oxford, 1661–1713," *RES,* XIX (Oct., 1943), 366–75; Wood, II, 165.

22. L.C. 5/140, p. 263; Ward, p. 10; Gardner, p. 558. See also C. E. Ward, *The Life of John Dryden,* 1961, p. 100.

23. Nicoll dates Duffett's *Empress* c. December, 1673, perhaps because the first edition was advertised in the Term Catalogues for May, 1674. But it is clearly a vacation play, probably presented in August, 1673.

24. Downes, p. 34; Hugh Macdonald, *John Dryden, a Bibliography,* 1939, p. 207; W. S. Clarke, "Pordage's *Herod and Mariamne,*" *RES,* V (1929), 61–4.

25. Nicoll, p. 443; J. H. Wilson, "Six Restoration Play-Dates," *N&Q,* N.S. 9, No. 6 (June, 1962), 221.

26. Hotson, p. 258.

27. Gardner, p. 60; *Williamson,* I, 180–1.

III. The War of the Theatres pages 33–48

1. Hooke, p. 131; L.C. 3/28, p. 201.

2. L.C. 3/28, p. 201. Clarke's name appears without date in a list of the King's servants in L.C. 2/24, between the names of Guilbert Soper and James Gray, who were sworn in on Sept. 11, 1674.

3. Cibber, II, 64, 316; Tobias Thomas, *The Life of the Late Famous Comedian Jo. Hayns*, 1701, p. 5.

4. *Williamson*, I, 180–1; Downes, p. 34; Nicoll, pp. 348, 356; Hooke, p. 108; William Van Lennep, "Nell Gwyn's Playgoing," *Harvard Library Bulletin*, IV, 3 (Autumn, 1950), 405–8.

5. *Letters of Humphrey Prideaux*, ed. E. M. Thompson, 1875, p. 5.

6. Nicoll, p. 345.

7. L.C. 5/141, p. 114, and Nicoll, p. 324.

8. Downes, p. 35; Settle's Preface to *Ibrahim*, 1677.

9. *Poems & Letters of Andrew Marvell*, ed. H. M. Margoliouth, 1927, II, 320; *Bulstrode*, I, 302; Evelyn, Sept. 29, 1675; Boswell, p. 121.

10. *CTB*, 1672–75, p. 826; *Bulstrode*, I, 305, 308.

11. Thomas Duffett, *New Poems, Songs, Prologues and Epilogues*, 1676, pp. 75–6.

12. Hooke, p. 177.

13. Hotson, p. 258.

14. Nicoll, pp. 324–5.

15. Nicoll, p. 325; L.C. 5/190, p. 134v.

16. L.C. 3/28, p. 201, and L.C. 3/24.

17. Nicoll, p. 346.

18. Rochester's "The Session of the Poets;" Downes, pp. 36–8.

19. L.C. 5/189, pp. 152, 182; L.C. 3/25, p. 263; L.C. 5/190, pp. 91, 92v, 106v, 115, 115v, 122v, 124, 132, 133, 134, 143, 164v, 166, 174, 174v. Many of these items are also listed by Nicoll, pp. 319–20.

20. Duffett's *Poems*, pp. 89–92; Thomas's *Hayns*, pp. 23, 35, 57, 61.

21. HMC, *Egmont* MS, II, 208.

22. Newdigate, Sept. 12, 1693; *Proceedings at the Old Bailey*, Oct. 12–17, 1695; Luttrell, III, 183, 205, 212, 445; William Egerton, *Faithful Memoirs of Mrs. Anne Oldfield*, 1731, p. 69.

23. P.R.O., S.P. 29/395, f. 33.

24. Cibber, II, 61, 63; HMC, *House of Lords MS*, II, 280; *State Trials*, XIII, 590–1; Wm. D. Montague, *Court and Society from Elizabeth to Anne*, 1864, II, 95–6.

25. L.C. 5/190, pp. 171, 172v.

IV. The Lean Years pages 49–64

1. L.C. 5/191, p. 5v; *The True Countess of Banbury's Case*, 1696; Luttrell, IV, 169; P.R.O., Court of Delegates, 212/494.

2. Charles Gildon, *The Laws of Poetry*, 1721, p. 38: " 'Tis true that after the Restoration, when the two houses struggled for the favor of

the town, the taking poets were secured to either house by a sort of retaining fee, which seldom or never amounted to more than forty shillings a week."

3. See A. F. White, *John Crowne*, 1922, pp. 34–5; Preface to *The Works of the Earls of Rochester, Roscomon, and Dorset*, 1731; HMC, *Rutland MS*, II, 36.

4. Downes, p. 16.

5. *Savile Correspondence*, ed. W. D. Cooper, 1858, p. 58 (June 5, 1677); L.C. 3/24; L.C. 3/28, p. 203; Wilson, pp. 120, 132, 154.

6. *CTB*, 1676–79, p. 397; Downes, p. 36.

7. *CSPD*, 1677, pp. 108, 117; P.R.O., S.P. 29/393, f. 112.

8. L.C. 5/142, p. 98; L.C. 5/190, p. 178; Sybil Rosenfeld, "Some Notes on the Players at Oxford," *RES*, XIX (October, 1943), 366–75.

9. L.C. 5/142, p. 98.

10. Hotson, pp. 259, 261-2, 269; P.R.O., Chancery 7/194/57.

11. Ward, p. 12; Wilson, pp. 134–5.

12. Boswell, p. 123; *The Rochester-Savile Letters*, 1941, ed. J. H. Wilson, p. 53.

13. J. M. Osborn, *Dryden Facts and Problems*, 1940, pp. 188-9; Fitzgerald, I, 145.

14. L.C. 5/191, p. 13v.

15. P.R.O., Court of Delegates, 212/494, p. 675. About 1697, before the Court of Delegates, Mrs. Boutell said of herself that she "hath been married to her husband Barnaby Bowtell sonne of Barnaby Bowtell of Parham Hall in Suffolk Esquire for about Twenty seaven yeares and her husband is a Lieut in King Williams army, where he now is." A commission for Mr. Barnaby Bowtell to be a lieutenant in Captain William LLoyd's company is listed in *CSPD*, 1697, p. 47 (March 1, 1697).

16. L.C. 5/143, p. 69.

17. L.C. 5/190, pp. 180, 182; L.C. 5/191, pp. 5v, 7, 8, 9v, 10, 13v, 16v.

18. Osborn, *Dryden Facts and Problems*, pp. 188-9; C. E. Ward, *Life of John Dryden*, 1961, p. 128, dates this petition in "the weeks following the performance of *All for Love* and before the acting of *The Kind Keeper*." However, the statement that Lee "has been in pension with us to the last day of our playing"—i.e., the end of the spring term—clearly suggests the summer of 1678. For the date of *Oedipus* see J. H. Wilson, "Six Restoration Play-Dates," *N&Q*, N.S. 9, No. 6 (June, 1962), p. 222.

18A. L.C. 3/28, p. 201.

19. *CTB*, 1676–79, pp. 1160, 1230; I. K. Fletcher, "Italian Comedians

in England in the 17th Century," *Theatre Notebook*, VIII (1954), 88–9.

20. Roger North, *Examen*, 1740, p. 238; *Middlesex County Records*, IV, 95; Langbaine, p. 366; P.R.O., S.P. 29/408, f. 64.

21. L.C. 5/191, pp. 31, 31v.

22. Hotson, p. 262.

V. Decline and Fall pages 65–81

1. Pepys, Dec. 8, 1666. The King saw two plays by the King's Company at Whitehall in February and March, 1679 (L.C. 5/143, p. 435). Thereafter he saw none at either theatre until 1681.

2. James C. Didbin, *Annals of the Edinburgh Stage*, 1888, pp. 26–8; Hotson, p. 262; L.C. 5/143, pp. 305, 394; L.C. 3/28, p. 201; Dryden's "Prologue to the University of Oxford," 1680, Gardner, p. 97.

3. Hotson, pp. 263, 268; L.C. 5/143, p. 399. Wintershall was buried on July 8, 1679 (*Registers of St. Paul's, Covent Garden*, IV, 84).

3A. See Kenneth M. Cameron, "Strolling with Coysh," *Theatre Notebook*, XVII, 1 (Autumn, 1962), 12–16.

4. Hotson, p. 262; P.R.O., Chancery 8/262/26.

5. *True News*, Feb. 4–7, 1679/80; Julia Cartwright, *Sacharissa*, 1901, pp. 224, 234; *Theatre Notebook*, XV, 3, 80; Luttrell, I, 34–5, 36, 41.

6. For the date of *Thyestes* see J. H. Wilson, "Six Restoration Play-Dates," *N&Q*, N.S. 9, No. 6, p. 222.

7. Hotson, pp. 264–5; P.R.O., Chancery 7/133/82.

8. *Theatre Notebook*, XV, 3, 80.

9. L.C. 5/143, pp. 506, 509; L.C. 7/1; HMC, *Ormonde Papers*, N.S. V, 320, 338.

10. Wood, II, 490; Nicoll, pp. 306–7.

11. Hotson, pp. 272–3; P.R.O., Chancery 24/1070/63.

12. Tate, *Poems Written on Several Occasions*, 1684, p. 153.

13. See Tate's "Epistle to the Readers;" Nicoll, p. 434; *Theatre Notebook*, XV, 3, 80; L.C. 5/144, p. 207.

14. *True Protestant Mercury*, March 19–23, 1681; Smith's *Protestant Intelligencer*, March 28, 1681; *Theatre Notebook*, XV, 3, 80.

15. Lucas, p. 266; Cibber, II, 63.

16. HMC, *House of Lords MS*, N.S. II, 280.

17. Additional MS. 27,277, f. 126v, "Warrant Book of Charles II."

18. L.C. 5/191, pp. 61, 80, 89v.

19. Gardner, p. 115. For the date of *The Unhappy Favourite* see J. H. Wilson, "Six Restoration Play-Dates," *N&Q*, N.S. 9, No. 6, p. 222.

20. Hotson, pp. 266–7; prologues prefixed to Ravenscroft's *Titus*

Andronicus, 4to, 1687; W. S. Clarke, *The Early Irish Stage*, 1955, p. 85.

21. L.C. 7/1, pp. 14, 15; L.C. 5/151, p. 131; L.C. 7/3; Charles Gildon, *History of the English Stage*, 1741, pp. 10–11.

22. Wiley, p. 40; *Loyal Protestant*, Oct. 29, 1681; Harvard MS. Eng. 633, p. 7, "Satyr to Julian."

23. Davies, II, 238–9. The date is debatable, but November seems the more likely time.

24. *Theatre Notebook*, XV, 3, 80; Newdigate, Feb. 4, 1682; *Loyal Protestant*, Feb. 23, 1682; *CSPD*, 1682, pp. 24, 28. The play on Jan. 14 is called simply "Caius Martius."

25. "To Madam Gwin A Rhymeing Supplication by Way of Ballad," Additional MS. 27,407, ff. 60–61v; HMC, *MS of Lord Montague of Beaulieu*, p. 182; L.C. 5/144, p. 274.

26. *Covent Garden Drollery* (1672), ed. George Thorn-Drury, 1928, pp. 34–5, 83–4. D'Urfey also used the prologue as the epilogue to his *The Fool Turn'd Critick*, 1676.

27. *Theatre Notebook*, XV, 3, 80.

28. Hotson, pp. 268, 270–3; Wiley, pp. 126–8.

29. *Theatre Notebook*, XV, 3, 81; *The Loyal Protestant*, Oct. 17, 1682; *Memoirs of Sir John Reresby*, 1936, p. 259.

VI. Barbara pages 82–96

1. Gardner, pp. 129–32; Luttrell, I, 62; Nicoll, pp. 365–6; W. S. Clarke, *The Early Irish Stage*, 1955, pp. 88–9; Sybil Rosenfeld, *The Theatre of the London Fairs*, 1960, p. 6.

2. *Poems on Affairs of State*, 1705, p. 144; Robert Gould, "The Playhouse. A Satyr," Additional MS. 30, 492.

3. Downes, p. 40.

4. Cibber, II, 64; Hotson, pp. 271–2; Harleian MS. 7319, ff. 281–94.

5. Abel Boyer, *History of the Life and Reign of Queen Anne*, Appendix, p. 48; Pepys, May 15, 1663; *Poems on Affairs of State*, 1705, p. 265.

6. Sergeant, pp. 222, 227; Harleian MS. 7006, ff. 171v, 175v–6.

7. Newdigate, April 8, Nov. 25, 1679; HMC, *Buccleuch* MS, I, 331; Cartwright, p. 273; Sergeant, p. 243; Luttrell, I, 178; *The Loyal Protestant*, May 11, 1682; E. F. Ward, *Christopher Monck Duke of Albemarle*, 1915, p. 169.

8. Sergeant, p. 188; Epilogue to Crowne's *The Ambitious Statesman*, 1679.

9. G. S. Thomson, *Life in a Noble Household*, ed. of 1959, p. 202; Lucas, p. 266.

10. Additional MS. 30,492, f. 28.
11. P.R.O., S.P. 29/438, p. 71; Newdigate, Sept. 4, Oct. 28, 1684; HMC, Twelfth Report, *House of Lords MS*, I, 304.
12. Additional MS. 10,117 (Rugge's "Mercurius Redivivus"), f. 53v.
13. P.R.O., S.P. 44/56, p. 136; *CSPD*, 1684–5, p. 172.
14. *CSPD*, 1684–5, p. 180; Newdigate, Oct. 21, 1684; J. C. Jeaffreson, *A Young Squire of the Seventeenth Century*, 1878, II, 143.
15. *CSPD*, 1684–5, p. 183; Luttrell, I, 318.
16. Newdigate, Nov. 8, 25, 1684; Luttrell, I, 317, 322; *The Arraignment, Tryal, and Condemnation of Peter Cooke*, 1696, p. 42; *State Trials*, XIII, 388.
17. P.R.O., S.P. 44/335, pp. 440–1; *CTB*, 1681–85, p. 1524.
18. *Tryal of Peter Cooke*, 1696, p. 65.

VII. Libels and Lampoons pages 97–110

1. L.C. 5/145, pp. 153, 184; Luttrell, I, 339; Downes, p. 40.
2. L.C. 5/147, pp. 24, 68–9.
3. P.R.O., S.P. 44/336, p. 260.
4. Choyce Collection, p. 159; Additional MS. 29,497, p. 42, and Harleian MS. 6914, p. 109.
5. HMC, *Downshire MS*, I, 135, 138, 140, 169; HMC, *Rutland MS*, II, 107, 110.
6. HMC, *Rutland MS*, II, 104.
7. Mary De la Riviere Manley, *The New Atalantis*, 1736, II, 22, 25.
8. "Tunbridge Satyr," Stowe MS. 969, p. 45.
9. Harleian MS. 7317, p. 106; *Poems on Affairs of State*, 1705, p. 352; G. S. Steinman, *Memoir of Barbara, Duchess of Cleveland*, 1871, p. 190.
10. See *The Night Walker*, October, 1696; Additional MS. 36,916, f. 62; Evelyn, Jan. 24, 1682; "The Haymarket Hectors," *Poems on Affairs of State*, 1716, III, 60–62; Dorset, *A Faithful Catalog of Our Most Eminent Ninnies*, c. 1683.
11. Lucas, p. 367; Davies, II, 238–9; Cibber, I, 183.
12. HMC, *Rutland MS*, II, 104.
13. See *Early Science in Oxford*, 1935, ed. R. T. Gunther, p. 111; Lucas, p. 267.
14. Ward, p. 27; HMC, *Buccleuch MS*, II, 97; HMC, *Rutland MS*, II, 103; HMC, *Downshire MS*, I, 116; Luttrell, II, 189, III, 475; *CSPD*, 1686, p. 28.
15. Choyce Collection, p. 280, and Harleian MS. 7317, p. 154. The satire must have been written after March 19, 1688, when the Duke of

NOTES 145

Grafton and Capt. Duncan Abercromy returned from a voyage in the Mediterranean.

16. Choyce Collection, p. 229.

17. Gould, *Poems*, 1709, II, 252. The version in his *Poems*, 1689, is very like that of the MS of 1684.

18. Sergeant, p. 271.

19. HMC, *House of Lords MS*, N.S. II, 280; *CSPD*, 1696, p. 142.

VIII. To Kill a King pages 111–127

1. Ailesbury, II, 374; Newdigate, April 6, Jan. 10, 13, 1693; *Portledge*, June 19, 1693, p. 163; *Proceedings at the Old Bailey*, May 31–June 8, 1693.

2. Additional MS. 29,497, p. 201.

3. Newdigate, Oct. 16, 1695; Luttrell, III, 484; *The Post Boy*, June 11–13, 1695.

4. *The Post Boy*, July 2–4, July 6–9, July 9–11, Oct. 15–17, 1695; Luttrell, III, 487, 494–5; HMC, *Downshire MS*, I, Pt. 2, 540; Sloane MS. 4460, f. 43.

5. *State Trials*, XIII, 607; Ailesbury, I, 354; N. de L'Hermitage, Additional MS. 34,491, f. 96v.

6. *Life of Major John Bernardi*, 1729, p. 128; Richard Blackmore, *True and Impartial History*, 1723, p. 98.

7. *The Post Boy*, Feb. 22–5, Feb. 27–9, March 7–10, 1696; HMC, *Fifth Report*, p. 385; N. de L'Hermitage, Additional MS. 34,491, f. 96v; Additional MS. 28,880, f. 241.

8. Gilbert Burnet, *History of His Own Times*, 1873, IV, 303: Luttrell, IV, 29, 30, 40, 46, 52.

9. Cardigan, *Life and Loyalties of Thomas Bruce*, 1951, pp. 122, 192; Ailesbury, II, 381; Vernon, I, 41; *CSPD*, 1696, pp. 109, 135. Twenty-four of Cooke's letters are in Lambeth MS. 1029.

10. Luttrell, IV, 52; *CSPD*, 1696, p. 107; Ailesbury, I, 353; *State Trials*, XIII, 362, 607; *Tryal of Peter Cooke*, 1696, p. 44.

11. Lambeth MS. 942/120.

12. Harleian MS. 7171; *CSPD*, 1696, pp. 135, 142, 147, 187; Luttrell, IV, 46, 52, 242; *Tryal of Peter Cooke*, 1696, p. 36.

13. *CSPD*, 1696, pp. 181, 197; Additional MS. 40,782, ff. 79v, 87v; P.R.O., L.C. 5/151, pp. 437–8.

14. Lambeth MS. 953/52; Additional MS. 40,782, ff. 89, 92v; *CSPD*, 1696, p. 142.

15. Luttrell, IV, 56; *London Newsletter*, May 29–June 1, 1696; *CSPD*, 1696, p. 223.

16. Additional MS. 40,060, f. 4.
17. Cibber, II, 62–3.
18. *Portledge*, p. 234; *State Trials*, XIII, 590; Harleian MS. 7171, pp. 163–65.
19. Ailesbury, II, 390–1, 400–1; for a variant of this story, in which O'Brian is said to have persuaded Goodman to flee by mixing threats with bribes, see Wm. D. Montague, *Court and Society from Elizabeth to Anne*, 1864, II, 95–6; HMC, *Downshire MS*, I, Pt. 2, 703, 740; Vernon, I, 40.

IX. Epilogue pages 128–135

1. Luttrell, IV, 137, 176; HMC, *House of Lords MS*, N.S. II, 214, 296; *A Letter Concerning the Attainder and Execution of Sir John Fenwick*, 1706.
2. Ailesbury, II, 368–9, 396, 431, 451; Luttrell, IV, 241, 250, 497, 523, V, 56; *Portledge*, pp. 222, 229.
3. *The Post Man*, Dec. 24–6, 1696; *The Post Boy*, May 15–18, 1697; Luttrell, IV, 182; C. E. Lart, *Jacobite Extracts from the Parochial Registers of St. Germain-en-Laye*, 1910, p. 120.
4. James Macpherson, *Original Papers*, 1775, I, 573; Luttrell, IV, 340, 347; HMC, *Bath MS*, III, 194, 198; *The Flying Post*, May 14–17, 1698.
5. Macpherson, *Original Papers*, 1775, I, 573.
6. Ailesbury, II, 398; Luttrell, IV, 529, 560.
7. Ailesbury, II, 482, 487, 491, 523; Luttrell, IV, 574, 598, 635.
8. Additional MS. 10,060, f. 10v.
9. Newdigate, July 25, 1706; *The Wentworth Papers*, ed. J. J. Cartwright, 1883, p. 58; Luttrell, VI, 70.
10. Luttrell, VI, 71, 94; Newdigate, Oct. 5, 1706; Harleian MS. 5805, f. 135.
11. *A Full and True Account of the Examination and Condemnation of Handsome Fielding*, 1706; Abel Boyer, *History of the Life and Reign of Queen Anne*, 1722, Appendix, p. 48; *State Trials*, XIV, 1327–72; *Dictionary of National Biography*, s.a. Fielding.
12. Lucas, p. 268; Ailesbury, II, 399; Charles T. Gatty, *Mary Davies and the Manor of Ebury*, n.d., I, 207, 214. During the war Forrester had traveled as governor to Sir Richard Grosvenor, but the couple had not, of course, been in France. Thomas Grosvenor of Eaton, Cheshire, born 1693, inherited the baronetage from his older brother Richard (1689–1732) in July, 1732, and died at Naples, Jan. 31, 1733.

Index

Abercromy, Duncan, 103-4, 105
Ailesbury, Robert Bruce, Earl of, 6, 8, 111-12, 114, 119, 121, 122, 126, 131, 135
Amorous Old Woman, The, 31
Amadei, Alexander, 91, 92, 93, 94, 122
Anne, Princess and Queen, 131, 132, 134
Ariane, 38
Arlington, Henry Bennet, Earl of, 87
Arnold, John, 68
Arran, James Douglas, Earl of, 107
Arrowsmith, Joseph,
  The Reformation, 30
Aston, Tony, 36
Aubrey, John, 33

Baden, Robert, 61
Baker, Katherine (actress), 53
Baker, Nicholas, 123
Banbury, Charles Knollys, Earl of, 49
Bancroft, John,
  The Tragedy of Sertorius, 63
Banks, John,
  The Rival Kings, 56
  The Destruction of Troy, 62
  The Unhappy Favourite, 74
Bannister, John, 54
Barclay, Sir George, 116-17, 129
Barry, Elizabeth (actress), 83, 84, 104, 125

Bateman, Sir Anthony, 54
Bates, Mrs. (actress), 53
Behn, Aphra, 58,
  The Feign'd Curtizans, 65
  The False Count, 77
  The Roundheads, 77
Beeston, George (actor), 35
Bell, Richard (actor), 14, 44
Bellasyse, Susanna, Lady, 105
Belon, Peter,
  The Mock-Duellist, 40
Bernardi, Major John, 116, 129
Bertie, Peregrine, 99, 103
Berwick, James Fitzjames, Duke of, 115
Betterton, Thomas (actor), 2, 12, 14, 82, 84, 85, 125
Blood, Col. Thomas, 74
Boutell, Elizabeth (actress), 17, 39, 51, 53, as Cleopatra, 58; retires, 60; returns to the stage, 104
Bracegirdle, Anne, 125
Bradley, John (tailor), 23
Brome, Richard,
  The Beggars' Bush, 32
Buckingham, George Villiers, Duke of, 9, 27,
  The Rehearsal, 29, 36
Buley, Betty, 30
Bulkeley, Henry, 105
Bulkeley, Sophia, 105
Burt, Nicholas (actor), 13, 22, 57, 61, 66, 76, 83

Cardell, Anne, 3
Cardell, Grace, 3
Cardell, Thomas, 3
Carlell, Lodowick,
   Arviragus and Philicia, 19
Cartwright, William, 13, 39, 42, 43, 54, 66, 76, dies, 83
Caryll, John,
   Sir Salomon, 67
Castlemaine, Roger Palmer, Earl of, 86, 106, 117, 132
Catherine, Dowager Queen, 1, 17, 27
Chamberlayne, William,
   Wits Led by the Nose, 55
Charles II, 7, 14, 15, 17, 19, 27, 39, 40, 132, grants players autonomy, 56; fights to save throne, 65; orders an inventory, 66; dissolves Parliament, 72; pardons Goodman, 73; returns to the theatre, 78; dissolves the King's Company, 80; with the Duchess of Cleveland, 87; orders Goodman prosecuted, 92; dies, 97
Charnock, Robert, 116, 119, 122
Charlton, Peter (actor), 41
Chatillon, Alexis Henry, Marquis de, 87
Cibber, Colley, 9, 12, 35, 48, 73, 102, 110, 124–5
Clarke, Thomas (actor), 23, 35, 41, 55, 74, 77, 78, 83, aids highwaymen, 47–8; a sharing actor, 69
Cleaver, Dr. William, 49
Cleveland, Barbara Palmer, Duchess of, at Cambridge, 7; at the theatre, 1, 27, 87; her extravagance, 28, 95; gambling, 28, 87; her history, 85–7; supposed child of, 100; characterized, 107–8; dismisses Goodman, 117; dares not admit him, 124; marries Fielding, 132; has him arrested, 133; marriage anulled, 134; dies, 134
Clun, Walter (actor), 22
Cooke, Peter, 95, 119, 120, tried, 121; convicted and banished, 122; dies, 129
Cooke, Sarah (actress), 53, 57, 67, 69, 71, 77, 78, 83, 84
Coppinger, Matthew, 47
Corbett, Mary (actress), 53, 74, 77

Cordell, Lowde, 10
Corey, Katherine (actress), 53, 58, 70, 78, 83
Cosmo de Medici, Prince, 6
Coysh, John (actor), 23, 35, 38, 41, 45, 55, 77, 78, coaches amateurs, 46; in Scotland, 67; turns to strolling, 83
Cox, Elizabeth (actress), 52, 58, 76, 77, 78, 83, 104
Cresswell, "Mother," 30
Cross, Mrs. Anne, 73, 128
Crowne, John, 37, 50,
   Charles the Eighth, 16
   Destruction of Jerusalem, 50, 51, 61, 78
   Calisto, 50
   The Ambitious Statesman, 64
   Thyestes, 68
   The Misery of Civil War, 69
Cuffly, Mrs., 104
Currer, Elizabeth (actress), 83

Davenant, Charles, 58, 80,
   Circe, 54
Davenant, Dame Mary, 14, 22
Davenant, Sir William, 14
Davies, Thomas, 102
Davis, Mary (actress), 27, 105
Davis, William, "the Golden Farmer," 47
Deleau, Mrs. Anne, 132
Dennis, John, 20, 25
Dighton, Christopher, 125, 128
Disney, Thomas (actor), 57, 69, 74, 78, 83
Dorchester, Katherine Sedley, Countess of, 105, 114
Dorset (Buckhurst), Charles Sheffield, Earl of, 27, 36, 102
Dover, John,
   The Mall, 31
Downes, John (prompter), 1, 39, 54, 84, 97
Draghi, Giovanni Battista, 37, 39
Dryden, John, 15, 19, 26, 29, 30, 32, 54, 59, 67, 68, 70, 72, 82, 103, 112,
   Marriage à la Mode, 16
   Secret Love, 17
   The Assignation, 18
   Amboyna, 21
   Sir Martin Mar-all, 31

INDEX

149

The Mistaken Husband, 31
Aurenge-Zebe, 42
The Indian Emperour, 46, 67
All for Love, 58
The Kind Keeper, 59
Oedipus, 61
Albion and Albanius, 97
Dudley, Capt. Dick, 47
Duffett, Thomas, 40, 54,
The Spanish Rogue, 19
The Empress of Morocco, 29–30, 33
The Mock-Tempest, 38
Psyche Debauch'd, 41
D'Urfey, Thomas, 23, 44,
Sir Barnaby Whigg, 8, 77
The Siege of Memphis, 44
Fool Turn'd Critick, 44
A Fond Husband, 52
Trick for Trick, 60
The Injured Princess, 80
The Boarding School, 126
Dutton, John, 63
Duval, Claude, 41, 47

Eastland, Edward (bookkeeper), 45, 61
Edwards (alias Douglas), 120
Etherege, Sir George, 103,
The Man of Mode, 44

Fane, Sir Francis,
Love in the Dark, 40
Farlowe, Mrs. (actress), 53
Fell, James, 123
Fenwick, Lady Mary, 126
Fenwick, Sir John, 73, 108, 114, 119, 120, 122, 125, 131, captured, 123; attainted and executed, 128–9
Fielding, Robert, Major General, 50, 132–4
Fiorelli, Tiberio ("Scaramouche"), 20, 29, 40–1
Fisher, Capt. Richard, 117
Fitzroy, Barbara, 86, 107
Forrester, Mr. 135
Freind, Sir John, 119, 122

Germaine, Sir John, 105
Gifford, Madam, 30
Gildon, Charles, 109
Gisborne, John, 117

Godfrey, Edmond, 73, 128
Godfrey, Sir Edmund Bury, 62
Golding, Daniel (housekeeper), 71
Goodman, Cardell, birth, 5; at college, 6; fables about him, 10–12; comes to London, 12; joins King's Company, 21; at Oxford, 29, 38; first role, 29; sworn in, 33, 43; poverty, 35; in *Julius Caesar*, 44; debts, 45; charged with highway robbery, 48; and Elizabeth Price, 49–50; in *The Rival Queens*, 51; in *The Country Innocence*, 52; in *Scaramouche*, 54; in *Wits Led by the Nose*, 55; in *The Rival Kings*, 56; signs with Killigrew, 57; in *King Edgar*, 57; in *All for Love*, 58; in *Mithridates*, 59; arrested, 59; in *The Man of Newmarket*, 60; in *Trick for Trick*, 60; certificate renewed, 62; and Sarah Young, 63; in Scotland, 66, 67; a sharing actor, 69; charged with robbery, 72–4; epilogue to *Mithridates*, 76; and Betty Cox, 77; in *Sir Barnaby Whigg*, 77; in *The Loyal Brother*, 78; in *The Heir of Morocco*, 80; in *Constantine*, 84; in *Valentinian*, 84; in demand as Alexander, 84; intrigue with the Duchess of Cleveland, 88; gentleman of her horse, 89; arrested, 90; charged with attempted poisoning, 91; convicted, 95; freed, 96; at Tunbridge Wells, 100; acts gratis, 102–3; a duel, 103; libeled, 104–7; his wife, 108; praised, 109; a Jacobite, 111–12; in a riot, 114; a kidnap plot, 115; in Newgate, 117; pressed to be a witness, 119–21; testifies against Cooke, 121; against Fenwick, 123; bailed, 123; flees to France, 127; at St. Germain, 129–30; secured in southern France, 130; at Montelimar, 135
Goodman, Cardell, senior, 3–5
Goodman, John, of Cumberlow Green, 3
Goodman, John, of Ware, 3

INDEX

Goodman, Katherine, 4–5
Gould, Robert, 90, 107
Grafton, Henry Fitzroy, Duke of, 86, 87, 90, 93, 94, 99, 101, 104, 122, 132
Grafton, Isabella, Duchess of, 87, 105
Gray, James (actor), 66, 68
Griffin, Philip (actor), 22, 23, 30, 35, 38, 55, 57, 66, 67, 71, 74, 77, 83
Grosvenor, Thomas, 135
Gunning, Peter, 5
Guy, Henry, 95
Gwyn, Nell (actress), 9, 27, 37, 68, 78, 106

Hailes, Henry (scenekeeper), 23
Hall, Jacob, 86, 133
Hamilton, Col. James, 86
Hamilton, James, 107
Hancock, Thomas (actor), 34, 43
Harris, Henry (actor), 9, 14, 26, 83
Harris, William (actor), 30, 35, 41
Hart, Charles (actor), 2, 9, 13, 20, 22, 25, 28, 32, 34, 39, 42, 43, 44, 55, 61, 64, 66, as Alexander, 51; in *All for Love*, 58; in *Mithridates*, 59; last role, 60; agreement with the Duke's Company, 76; dies, 83
Hart, James, 37
Haynes, Joseph (actor), 9, 18, 22, 25, 35, 36, 38, 39, 41, 43, 55, 60, 64, 75, 83, 89, in debt, 45; in vacations, 46; as Harlequin, 54; suspended, 56; goes to Scotland, 66; returns, 79
Hinton, Mall, 104
Hind, Capt. James, 47
Hobbes, Thomas, 6, 8
Hodges, John, 47
Holt, Sir John, Chief Justice, 133
Hooke, Grace, 21
Hooke, John, 4
Hooke, Robert, 4, 12, 21, 22, 33, 37, 41, 44, 103
Holton, Mrs. (actress), 78, 83
Howard, Edward,
  The Man of Newmarket, 60
Howard, Mall, 104
Hughes, William (actor), 21, 45

Ingram, Major Robert, 126, 127

James II, 7, 20, 27, 65, 113, 125, at Edinburgh, 67; patronizes theatres, 97; pardons Goodman, 98; flight to France, 106; an exile, 111; at St. Germain, 129
James, Prince, "the Old Pretender," 113, 131
James, Elizabeth (actress), 39, 52
Jeffreys, George, Chief Justice, 92, 93
Jermaine, Mr. (actor), 67, 77, 78, 83
Jermyn, Henry, 86, 101
Jevon, Thomas (actor), 83
Johnson, Thomas, 61
Jolly, Thomas, 61
Julian, Robert, 99
Julius Caesar, 44, 84

Kent, Thomas (scenekeeper), 61
Keys, Thomas, 117
Kew, Nathaniel (actor), 23, 30
Killigrew, Charles, 12, 43, 55, 61, 66, 69, 78, 80, becomes Master, 51; forms new company, 56–7
Killigrew, Henry, 66, 69
Killigrew, Thomas, 12, 13, 14, 24, 26, 36, 39, 42, 43,
  The Parson's Wedding, 17
King, Sir Edmund, 119
Kirby, Christopher, 62
Kite, Thomas, 45
Knepp, Elizabeth (actress), 39, 41, 53, 70, 78
Knight, Ursula (actress), 53
Kynaston, Edward (actor), 13, 39, 42, 43, 44, 55, 58, 66, 80, 84, retires, 57; agreement with Duke's Company, 76; returns to the stage, 83

Lacy, John (actor), 13, 25, 36, 66, retires, 57; dies, 76; his widow, Margaret, 76
Lane, John, 78
Laytus, Bridget (mantua maker), 112
Leanerd, John,
  The Country Innocence, 52, 55
  The Rambling Justice, 59
  The Counterfeits, 61

INDEX 151

Lee, Nathaniel, 23, 61,
   The Rival Queens, 2, 51, 55, 69, 78, 84, 88
   The Tragedy of Nero, 38
   Sophonisba, 40, 71
   Gloriana, 43
   Mithridates, 59, 76, 103
   The Princess of Cleve, 77
   Constantine, 84
Leigh, Anthony (actor), 22, 83, 85
Leigh, Elinor (actress), 83
Lewsay, Mr., 109, 123
Lister, Margaret, 49
Locke, Matthew, 37, 39
Lucas, Theophilus, 3, 72, 73, 90, 102, 103, 134
Lucy, Capt. Thomas, 99
Lydall, Edward (actor), 34, 39, 41, 52, 55

Macaulay, Thomas, 3
Macbeth, 19, 29, 37, 70
Mackarel, Betty (orange-girl), 38
Maidwell, Lewis, 6,
   The Loving Enemies, 6
Manchester, Edward Montague, Earl of, 10
Manley, Mrs. Mary, 107–8, 109
Marlborough, John Churchill, Duke of, 86, 89, 101
Marsh, George, 108, 128
Marshall, Rebecca (actress), 17, 51, 52, 58
Mary (of Modena), Queen, 47, 81, 103, 106, 131
Mary (Stuart), Queen, 114
Mather, Robert (scenekeeper), 74
Mazarin, Hortense, Duchess de, 105
Medbourne, Matthew (actor), 63, 66
Meggs, Mrs. Mary (fruit-woman), 14, 23
Merchant, Mrs. (actress), 53
Middleton, Charles, Earl of, 130
Mohun, Michael (actor), 13, 15, 22, 25, 32, 39, 43, 44, 57, 61, 64, 66, 76, 78, in *All for Love*, 58; in *Mithridates*, 59; letter to Secretary Williamson, 63; dies, 83
Monmouth, James, Duke of, 9, 65, 67, 68, 97
Montague, Ralph, 86, 87

Montgomery, William Herbert, Viscount, 119, 120, 122, 129, 130
Morrice, George (scenekeeper), 67
Moseley, "Mother," 30
Mountfort, Susanna (actress), 42, 77, 78, 83
Mountfort, William (actor), 2, 103
Moyle, Mrs. (actress), 77, 78
Mulgrave, Ursula, Countess of, 105

Newcastle, William Cavendish, Duke of, 37
Nokes, James (actor), 83, 85
Norfolk, Mary Howard, Duchess of, 105
Northumberland, Catherine (Lucy), Duchess of, 99, 105
Northumberland, George Fitzroy, Duke of, 86, 93, 94, 99, 122

Oates, Titus, 6, 62, 63, 85
O'Brian, William, 48, 108, 123, 126, flees with Goodman, 127; at St. Germain, 129; secretary to Ailesbury, 131
Ormonde, James Butler, Duke of, 70
Otway, Thomas,
   Alcibiades, 42
   Titus and Berenice, 44, 50, 54
   Don Carlos, 44
   Cheats of Scapin, 54
   The Orphan, 102

Parker, Col. John, 50
Pate, Mr. (singer), 114
Payne, Henry Neville, 37,
   The Morning Ramble, 18
Pendergrasse, Capt. Thomas, 117, 123, 129
Pepys, Samuel, 26, 53
Percival, Susannah, see Mountfort
Percival, Thomas (actor), 47
Perkins, Sir William, 119, 122
Perin, Carey (actor), 23, 55, 57, 67, 69, 77, 78, 83
Perryman, Andrew (wardrobe-keeper), 71
Piso's Conspiracy, 41
Pordage, Samuel, 58,
   Herod and Mariamne, 30
Porter, Capt. George, 114, 115, 116, 119, 122, 123, 128, turns King's

evidence, 117; testifies against Cooke, 121; against Fenwick, 123; betrays suborners, 124; despised, 129
Porter, Thomas, 58
Portland, William Bentinck, Earl of, 130
Portsmouth, Louise Keroualle, Duchess of, 27, 69, 101
Powell, Martin (actor), 30, 35, 41, 45, 55, 57, 61, 77, 83, coaches amateurs, 46; in Scotland, 67; a sharing actor, 69; a prologue at Oxford, 81
Price, Mrs. Alice, 49, 61
Price, Elizabeth (actress), 49–50
Prior, Matthew, 83, 130

Quin, Anne (actress), 53, 74, 78

Ravenscroft, Edward, 75,
 Citizen Turn'd Gentleman, 16, 18
 Scaramouche, 53, 55
 King Edgar and Alfreda, 57
 The English Lawyer, 57
 Titus Andronicus, 62
 The London Cuckolds, 77
Redding, Balthazar (singer), 114, 123
Reeve, Anne (actress), 17
Reggio, Pietro, 37
Richmond, Frances Stuart, Duchess of, 105
Robins, John, 124
Roche, Elizabeth (actress), 66
Rochester, John Wilmot, Earl of, 8, 27, 29, 30, 31, 36, 86,
 Valentinian, 84
 Rollo, Duke of Normandy, 78
Rookwood, Brigadier Ambrose, 116
Rourke, Heleine, 130
Rourke, Hugues, 130
Rowe, Thomas, 114, 125–6, 128
Rue, Francis de la, 116, 123, 129
Rutland, Katherine Manners, Countess of, 103
Rutter, Margaret (actress), 52

St. Albans, Charles Fitzroy, Duke of, 106
St. Albans, Henry Jermyn, Earl of, 28

St. André (dancer), 37, 39
Salisbury, Frances Cecil, Countess of, 131
Sandford, Samuel (actor), 83
Saunders, Charles,
 Tamerlane the Great, 72
Saunders, Joseph, 127
Saunders, Richard (actor), 78, 83
Savile, Henry, 27, 86
Sawyer, Sir Robert, 93
Saywell, John, 5
Sedley, Sir Charles, 27, 36, 58
Settle, Elkanah, 39,
 The Empress of Morocco, 20, 29, 31
 Cambyses, 20
 The Female Prelate, 69, 70, 71
 Fatal Love, 71
 The Heir of Morocco, 79
Shadwell, Thomas,
 Epsom Wells, 19, 31
 Psyche, 39
 The Virtuoso, 44
 The Lancashire Witches, 77
Shaftesbury, Anthony Cooper, Earl of, 65, 85
Shatterall, Robert (actor), 13, 22, 39, 45, 61, 66, 76, retires, 83; his house, 91
Sheppey, Thomas (actor), 23, 35, 69, 83
Shipman, Thomas,
 Henry the Third of France, 16
Shirley, George (actor), 21
Silence, Mrs., 71
Silent Woman, The, 29
Skipwith, Sir Thomas, 125
Slade, Betty (actress), 52
Slingsby, Lady Mary (actress), 83
Smith, Daniel, 63
Smith, Matthew, 124
Smith, William (actor), 9, 82–3, 84, 85
Southampton, Charles Fitzroy, Duke of, 86
Southerne, Thomas,
 The Loyal Brother, 78
Stevenson (painter), 39
Stratford, Mrs., 71
Streeter, Robert, 12
Styles, Mr. (actor), 67

INDEX

Sunderland, Robert Spencer, Earl of, 91, 92, 95
Sussex, Anne Fitzroy, Countess of, 86
Sydserf, Thomas, 66, 75

Talbot, John, 104
Temple, "Sister," 30
Tenison, Archbishop Thomas, 119–20, 126
Tonge, Israel, 62
Toppe, Anne, 4
Toppe, John, 3
Torcy, Marquis de, 130
Treby, Sir John, Chief Justice, 122
Tudor, Lady Mary, 105

Underhill, Cave (actor), 83, 85
Uphill, Anne (actress), 52
Uphill, Susanna (actress), 52

Vernon, James, 121
Villars, Charlotte, 134
Vincent, Mrs. (actress), 53
Voto, Antonio di, 21, 41

Wadsworth, Mary, 134
Watson, Marmaduke (actor), 30, 34, 55, 57, 69, 83

William III, 3, 46, 50, 111, at Cambridge, 7; invited, 106; plans to kidnap him, 115; assassination plot, 116–17; offers reward for Goodman, 128; death, 131
Williams, Mr., 114
Wilson, Mrs., 108
Wiltshire, John (actor), 23, 35, 38, 55, 66, 91
Wintershall, William (actor), 13, 25, 42, 45, 66, 75
Wit without Money, 15
Wood, Anthony, 33
Wood, Robert, 70
Wren, Sir Christopher, 12, 22, 31
Wright, Henry (scenekeeper), 45, 61
Wyatt, Mrs. (actress), 52
Wycherley, William, 27, 86, 112, 133,
  The Country Wife, 39
  The Plain Dealer, 44, 72

York, Duke of, see James II
York, Duchess of, see Mary of Modena
Young, Nell, 12, 21
Young, Ralph, 92
Young, Sarah, 63, 77

www.ingramcontent.com/pod-product-compliance
Lightning Source LLC
Chambersburg PA
CBHW031250290426
44109CB00012B/519